Yours in Filial Regard

Yours in Filial Regard

THE CIVIL WAR LETTERS OF A TEXAS FAMILY

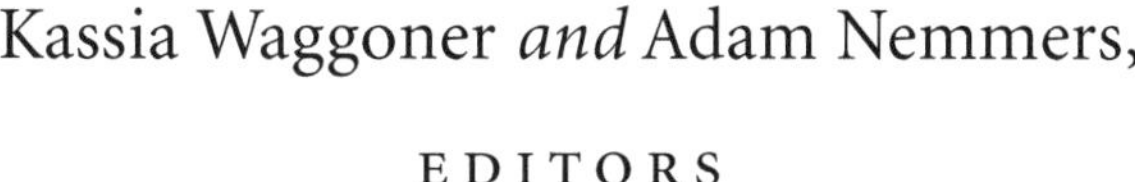

Kassia Waggoner *and* Adam Nemmers,

EDITORS

Library of Congress Cataloging-in-Publication Data

Love (Family : 1828 : Limestone County, Tex. : Love, James Marshall, 1805-1876), author.
[Correspondence. Selections]
Yours in filial regard: the Civil War letters of a Texas family / Kassia Waggoner and Adam Nemmers. -- Edition: first.
pages cm
Contains the text of letters found in the Love Family Letters archive, housed in the Special Collections Department of the Mary Couts Burnett Library, Texas Christian University, as well as an introduction which provides commentary.
Includes bibliographical references and index.
ISBN 978-0-87565-612-0 (alk. paper)
1. Love family--Correspondence. 2. Love family--Archives. 3. Soldiers--Texas--Correspondence. 4. Texas--History--Civil War, 1861-1865--Personal narratives, Confederate. 5. Texas--History--Civil War. 1861-1865--Social aspects. I. Waggoner, Kassia, editor. II. Nemmers, Adam, editor. III. Mary Couts Burnett Library. IV. Title.
E467.L682 2015
973.7'82092--dc23
[B]

2015000625

TCU Press
TCU Box 298300
Fort Worth, Texas 76129
817.257.7822
www.prs.tcu.edu

To order books: 1.800.826.8911

Designed by Barbara Mathews Whitehead

Contents

Foreword

BY THE TIME of the Civil War, people probably produced and read more letters than they did any other genre of writing. Exchanged in a variety of contexts ranging from interpersonal to business settings, letters were passed from hand to hand or through the mail, read out loud or silently devoured, treasured and passed down through generations, or, sometimes, burned. With the lowering of postal rates at several points in the nineteenth century, as well as the development of the postal system and the regional and national infrastructures necessary to support it, as many as 161 million letters passed through the US post office in 1861, according to historian David M. Henkin—up from 27 million only two decades earlier.[1] As numerous historians have noted, the Civil War prompted more letter writing than did any other national event in the nineteenth century. The distance war imposed between loved ones prompted heroic epistolary struggles to maintain relationships over long periods of separation. Letters helped close the distances separating correspondents through the exchange of news and sentiment, and allowed them to express their experiences of war on both the battlefield and the home front. Civil War letters still speak powerfully to readers today, as the continued publication of collections of such letters indicates.

The men and women who make up the Love family of north central Texas emerge as dutiful, witty, pious, and affectionate, as their voices come alive on the page a century and a half after they were first set on paper from battlefields and kitchen tables. This collection, *Yours in Filial Regard: The Civil War Letters of a Texas Family,* is unique in that it includes the correspondence of an extended family unit as they strived to maintain familial relationships during wartime. The editors of the following volume, Kassia Waggoner and Adam Nemmers, present a compelling account in their introduction of how this familial communications network, invented to overcome the disruptions war imposed on the exchange of letters, functioned during the years family members were separated. Little scholarly work has been done on how individuals maintained epistolary connections when the odds of doing so during wartime seem nearly insurmountable. Waggoner and Nemmers, through scrupulous research, careful transcription and annotation techniques, and sensitive interpretation, have put together a scholarly edition of significance to a number of academic fields, including Civil War history, Texas history, epistolary studies, American literature, and Southern studies. Just as important, they introduce readers to the extraordinary epistolary efforts undertaken by one family to maintain their familial bonds and identity in the face of separation, trials, and tragedy.

Waggoner and Nemmers discovered the Love family letters in TCU's Special Collections while working on a class assignment for a graduate class I taught on early American epistolary writings, a component of their doctoral coursework in the TCU Department of English. The course explored the emerging field of epistolary studies, an interdisciplinary endeavor practiced by historians and literary scholars who investigate the cultural, social, political, and aesthetic significance of letters in their historical contexts, and incorporated training in documentary editing and archival methodologies. When I read the edition of letters Waggoner and Nemmers collaboratively prepared and the introduction they had jointly written for their final project, I was struck both by the originality and sophistication of their argument about the family communications network and by the historical significance of the documents with which they worked. I watched with amazement and pride as they continued the project after the class concluded, eventually seeking and achieving publication with TCU Press. An accomplishment that displays the ability to sense when texts bear significance for broader audiences and the dedication and tenacity to see a project through to its completion and publication, bringing this edition to print is an impressive and unusual achievement for two young scholars at the outset of their academic careers. It is also a gift to readers, allowing us to encounter these fascinating and moving letters in the comfort of our armchairs at home rather than bent over a library table in an archive, striving to read the unfamiliar handwriting or make sense of obscure references. Editors of letter collections like this one perform an important service to academic and broader communities by making historical documents available, and for this work, Waggoner and Nemmers are to be thanked and congratulated.

Theresa Strouth Gaul
Professor of English
Texas Christian University
Author of To Marry an Indian

1. David M. Henkins, *The Postal Age: The Emergence of Modern Communications in Nineteenth-Century America* (Chicago: University of Chicago Press, 2006).

Editorial Method

THE LOVE FAMILY LETTERS collection, located in Special Collections of Mary Couts Burnett Library at Texas Christian University, was generously donated to TCU by Robert R. Van Vleck of Fort Worth, Texas, who discovered the letters at a yard sale. The letters were immediately treated and placed in protective sleeves, and have since been numbered, scanned, and digitized for the TCU collection. In all, there are seventy-three numbered letters in the collection and about ten uncategorized pieces, mostly envelopes and letter fragments, spanning the years 1859 through 1866, with the bulk written during the war years of 1861-64. To the best of our ability, we have placed the unnumbered fragments into the collection where they best match contextually and thematically, which brings the total of our comprehensive volume to eighty-two letters. We have indicated within the document, using headnotes and line breaks, which letters have been inserted into the sequence. As a result of these changes, the order of the letters in this book differs from the numbering system used in the archives. As much as possible (including in the Introduction) we have striven to maintain the integrity and intent of the Love family letters, reproducing their phrasing, punctuation, and spelling verbatim, with the following concessions to ensure readability for a modern audience:

- We use [?] to indicate a word that is illegible or requires further verification.
- We use [word] for an educated guess.
- We have footnoted material conditions such as tears in the page, folds, or blacked-out portions of the letter, insofar as they interfere with the readability of the text. Other material conditions of interest, such as

peculiar instances where pencil was used instead of ink, are also mentioned in notes.

- If a word or phrase was written above the line of the page we use ^word^ to indicate the start and stop of the insertion.
- Letters that were appended above the line at the end of words (usually possessives, abbreviations, and plurals) have been superscripted.
- We have used §§ to indicate marks Sam apparently used for emphasis, which look more like 33EE.
- We use curly brackets {{ to indicate when Sam or Cyrus use parallel vertical lines or other symbols before and after a phrase.
- When two parallel horizontal dashes are used, we supply an equal symbol [=]. The authors often use these as parentheses or a dash.
- We have maintained original capitalizations, spelling, punctuation, and underlines.
- We have maintained editorial markings such as crossed-out words (if legible) and footnoted instances where the words marked out are illegible.
- We did not maintain original line or page breaks with the exception of one letter in the collection, which includes an explanatory headnote.
- The placement of the date, origin, addressee, salutation, and closing in the original letters is varied and generally unorthodox. Although in the originals such variations are visually interesting, they are not well replicated in type, so these elements have been given more uniform placement in this text.

We hope these methods improve the accessibility of the collection.

Introduction

The Love Family Letters archive exhibits a broad communication network consisting of writers on both home and war fronts, spanning the entirety of the Civil War. The Loves were a prominent family in Texas, many holding political office after the war, and their experiences are of historical significance to residents of the greater Dallas-Fort Worth area and to Texans in general. The breadth and depth of this collection represents a significant addition both to epistolary studies and to the literature of the Civil War.

Seventy-nine of the letters in this volume are written by the soldiering Love brothers—Cyrus, Sam, James, and John Love, and brother-in-law John Karner—to their parents and siblings in Texas. In addition, the collection preserves three letters sent between women on the home front. Beyond the extant letters, there is ample evidence to suggest that Eliza Terrisa Love (Tea), Mary Elizabeth Love Karner (Bettie or Betty), Ellen Love, Fannie Farnsworth, and Lou Karner, among others, wrote to the soldiers and to each other, establishing a complex, extensive network of correspondence from the home front to the various battlefields and back. Thus, the volume presented here is only a sample of a much larger body of epistles; absent, sadly, are letters that were received but not preserved and the untold number of letters that were damaged, miscarried, captured, or otherwise lost in the confusion of war.

At the time of the Civil War, Americans engaged in letter writing perhaps more than at any other time in American history. Many of these letters have survived and been preserved for posterity, allowing researchers invaluable access to primary accounts of the events that transpired. In his book *Letter Writing in America Before Telecommunications,* William Decker describes the importance of Civil War letters to epistolary studies as a whole:

> One measure of how widely practiced the genre had become by the second half of the nineteenth century is the abundance of surviving Civil War correspondence at every level of literary accomplishment and from every region, and the fact that so many exchanges between soldiers and their families were preserved and in some cases printed indicates a readiness to recognize in such documents writing of historical and moral value. (1998, 60)

Your Affectionate Son: Letters from a Civil War Soldier; An Uncommon Soldier: The Civil War Letters of Sarah Rosetta Wakeman; Love and War: The Civil War Letters and Medicinal Book of Augustus C. Ball; and *Letters Home to Sarah: The Civil War Letters of Guy C. Taylor* are but a few of such collections, most of which contain a single author's story. In general, collections of letters tend to concentrate on the correspondence sent by one person. Few include correspondence from a family unit or from the multiple fronts of the war.

Yours in Filial Regard is unique because it focuses on the lives of ordinary Confederate soldiers and includes letters written by a wide variety of authors, both male and female, soldier and citizen. In all, nine authors and at least nine named recipients are featured in this collection, providing a broad, multifaceted portrait of life for a Texan family during the Civil War. The letters are of historical significance because they reveal not only information about drills, battles, generals, and strategies, but also about domestic life for women at home in Texas, with glimpses of family duties, schooling, child rearing, and courtship. Yet we, like many scholars today (Gaul, Harris, Bannet, et al.), accord letters an independent literary status, and *Yours in Filial Regard* adds to those conversations. The letters are valuable from a literary and rhetorical standpoint because they reveal how authors constructed and delivered letters to their loved ones, demonstrating that soldiers were aware of the importance of letter writing and the multiple audiences that each letter had the potential to address. Moreover, this edition explores how the letters' recipients circulated and responded to the information therein. The letters tell of tensions between concepts of glory, honor, and death; the conflict between a soldier's duty and a brother's duty; the struggle to maintain communication among multiple siblings and parents (some of whom were not literate); and the effort to send good news or a hopeful message despite the horrors of war.

In presenting *Yours in Filial Regard: The Civil War Letters of a Texas Family,* we are confronted with a problem of plenty: multiple authors, multiple recipients, and an array of scholarly considerations—historical, rhetorical, epistolary—that accompany the text. The collection as a whole yields strong narrative elements: the soldiers' fates; family relationships and friendships; mis- and disinformation; charges of perfidy; and the enlistment of the youngest Love son. Like an absorbing Civil War novel, this volume presents realistic, thematic, and sentimental depictions of the war's reality at the front and at home.

ORIGINS[1]

Hailing from the White's Creek Community in the rolling hills of Nashville, Tennessee, the Loves of Limestone County came to Texas in 1836. Eight years previously, James Marshall Love married Terrisa Ade-

James Marshall Love,
the Love family patriarch.

line Braden, a union soon blessed with children: Joseph within a year after their marriage, followed in short order by Cyrus and Martha. The Loves had seven children in all by the time the family departed for Texas.

Like many of their compatriots, the Loves were beckoned westward by the promise of lax laws and free land. Compared to Tennessee, Texas would have been a remarkable change in landscape: largely flat and dry, still inhabited by significant Indian populations, and only sparsely settled by Europeans, especially in the northern plains, far from established towns along the Gulf Coast and Brazos River. Indeed, when the Loves' wagon train arrived in the fall of 1836, the territory had only recently been reopened for Anglo settlement after the stunning Texas Revolution—the population numbering fewer than 50,000, a good many of these Mexicans, American Indians, and enslaved Africans. During the

Terrisa Adeline Braden Love, the matriarch of the Love family.

first decade of the Loves' residence, Texas asserted itself as an independent nation, the Republic of Texas, under President Sam Houston, its population surging to over 125,000 by the time it was annexed to the United States in 1845.

Against this backdrop the family worked to establish a homestead near Tehuacana, in Limestone County northeast of Waco, clearing hundreds of acres for crops and raising many head of livestock, which were driven annually to market in New Orleans (the railroad would not arrive until after the Civil War). These were long, lonely days spent on the prairie, the large family growing larger with every year—James, Samuel, David, John—until the birth of Tennessee Angelina Love in 1849, the last of fifteen children born in twenty years, not all of whom survived. By all accounts the Loves were a close-knit and industrious family that soon became prominent in Limestone County, itself growing rapidly with the influx of Anglo settlers from east of the Mississippi.

As the years progressed, daughter Mary Elizabeth married and left the Love ranch for a homestead of her own. The family's eldest surviving son, Cyrus, moved to Fairfield where he, along with brother-in-law John Karner, established the Male and Female School in 1859. Keeping with common practice, the Loves likely maintained a weekly correspondence regarding family affairs, farm business, and town gossip, their letters often delivered by stagecoach lines executing government mail contracts. These domestic rhythms were soon to be disrupted by the beginning of the Civil War in 1861.

Though Texas had seceded from the Union in February and joined the Confederate States of America in March, it stayed out of active conflict during the Confederate capture of Fort Sumter in April and First Manassas (called the First Battle of Bull Run by the Union) in July. In the meantime public sentiment brewed; still the call to war did not reach Limestone County until finally, in late August of 1861, Governor Edward Clark issued a request for Confederate troops in a broadside, telling his citizens, "You require no appeal to animate your patriotism. . . . If you want a speedy peace, you must be prepared to conquer it" (Gilder Lehrman Collection). Once the call came, the Loves and other Limestone County boys answered immediately. ("Limestone County boys" are referred to frequently in the letters—*boys* referring to enlisted men throughout the correspondence.) Cyrus was the first to answer the call. Enlisting as a foot soldier, he joined Company G of the Seventh Texas Infantry under John Gregg of Fairfield. As was common with other families during the conflict, Cyrus was separated from his brothers Sam and John, who mustered into the Sixth Texas Cavalry in Dallas in September 1861. Although they enlisted at the same time and place, Sam and John were directed into different companies—Sam to G Company and John to F. James would later join the Twentieth Texas Cavalry, or Bass's Regiment, in the spring of 1862. Sam and John were sent to the Missouri border, Cyrus to Tennessee, and James to Arkansas. Calculating only according to the year (not the month), at the beginning of the war, Cyrus was thirty-one years old, James was twenty-five, Sam twenty-three, and John nineteen. Their youngest brother Robert, already eager to join the fight, was only fourteen.

"Now I Intend to Propose a Plan by Which You May All Hear from Me When I Am on the March as Well as for Me to Hear from You"

Initially the Love brothers have confidence in the Confederate postal system, as they take care to include detailed addresses and forwarding instructions in the body of their letters. Cyrus, in an early letter, tells his parents, "You can write to me at any time from where I write my letters to you and they will be forwarded to me at any other place I may have moved to" *(Letter 9)*. As John later explains, "We will get them by a direct path from there to our camps" *(Letter 14)*. As the war continued, however, official mail service became increasingly scattershot. Problems in the Confederate postal system and the hectic and unpredictable days of war prevented the soldiers from receiving as many letters as they wanted, or writing as many as family members expected.

Faced with problematic and unreliable mail service, the Loves used a correspondence network to share news, locate loved ones, assess welfare, and relay sentiments to correspondents at home and on the front. The genesis of this system is proposed by Sam in Letter 20, written early in the war, and adopted by Cyrus, John, and James thereafter. Sam's letter is significant for the following reasons: 1.) It explains why Sam is capable of writing only to a few specific people. 2.) It proposes the system and describes how it will work. 3.) It establishes a method for sharing letters with those outside the family who would also be interested in hearing from him. 4.) It explains from a soldier's perspective the importance both of writing letters and of receiving them.

In his letter, Sam first rationalizes why he is unable to send letters home to all his friends and relations: "If I dont write to all of you while I am on the march it is no fault of mine for it is all I can do to write atall. . . . So you see that it was not because I did not wish to write to you . . . but because I could not help it very well." He further explains that the letters he has managed to compose have been sent to Tea and his parents with the expectation that his other siblings and friends would "learn all from Teas and fathers letters . . . as well as how to direct your letters." Yet he realizes that his other siblings, Mary Elizabeth in particular, are hurt by this arrangement, so he attempts to rectify the situation by devising the following strategy: "And now I intend to propose a plan by which you may all hear from me when I am on the march as well as for me to hear from you. It is this I will write first to one and then to the other and when the one written to receives it you will seal it and send it to the other . . . both writing as soon as you receive it." Furthermore, he reveals that he intends his letters to be shared with several communities: "I cannot write to all of them in a different letter but where I have a number of friends in one town or neighborhood I could write to them all in one and by that means keep up a correspondence with several towns and neighborhoods and also keep them informed about what is going on here." Finally, he notes his need for both receiving and writing letters amidst the misery of war: "For my greatest pleasure is in receiving and reading letters . . . and all my friends seem to think that I should open a correspondence instead of Studying the disadvantages under which I labor" *(Letter 20).*

"My Love to the Family and All Enquiring Friends"

Although the Loves' arrangement is noteworthy, their family communication network was not the only one in place during the war. The letters reveal that Limestone County was close-knit, and that information found within one soldier's letter was likely read or shared with neighbors. This community network is revealed in the wealth of extrafamilial information regarding the Limestone County boys in letters written by Cyrus and Sam. The soldier's community allegiance extended into camp, as the boys likely read letters from home aloud to one another. For example, Sam tells Tea, "I was very sorry to hear of Ewing Caruthers.es deth. . . . You may be a little surprised about how I learned this so I will tell you. Ben.. Kenady got a letter from Mrs Wash Kenady about 10 days since" *(Letter 45).*

At times when the brothers are unable to write home themselves, they dictate to others capable of sending mail on their behalf. For example, when John Karner is incapacitated, he calls upon his friend William Blaine, who adds a postscript to Sam's letter to Bettie, assuring her of her husband's health. Likewise, when Cyrus falls ill, he asks his friends in his regiment to write home for him.

Sam draws our attention to an instance when others wrote home with unflattering rumors about camp life. His letter to Tea reveals his frustration that others are spreading gossip about him: "You stated in your last letter that you had heard of something that I had been guilty of some misconduct that was disgraceful. I would like to know what it is for I am not aware of anything that I have done that would have disgraced me at home even. I would like to know who was the kind informant" *(Letter 72)*. This letter demonstrates the strength of the community network, for good or ill. The fact that the Love brothers refer to themselves as a part of the Limestone County boys rather than using other markers of identification, like their company or regiment, is a testament to the power of their community ties.

THE LETTER-WRITING SOLDIER

When a soldier decides to write a letter, there are many factors that must be considered: his exigency and motivation in writing; the audience to whom he should write, and what topics to broach with which audience; with what materials he will compose; and how to deliver the letter once it is written. The Love brothers made conscious decisions regarding all these layers of communication.

"As We Have Halted This Evening . . . I Thought I Would Write You a Few Hasty Lines"

Letter-writing etiquette of the day dictated that a response be made to a letter soon after receipt. Any lack of response could be perceived as a lack of affection (Gerber 2006, 101). As members of an affluent family, the Loves would have been well trained in the etiquette of letter writing, and feel obligated to answer their family members. Sometimes, the occasion for writing is one of sudden opportunity rather than the result of deliberation: Sam and Cyrus often note that they are writing hastily after having learned that a bearer is headed to Texas.

The Love brothers wrote letters to share news and inquire about family and friends at home. On numerous occasions, Cyrus and Sam inquire about the stability of the farm. For example, Sam writes, "Tell me all about what is going on at home what all the people are doing what new improvements have been mad and particularly about the things about home how the sheep horses and cows are getting on" *(Letter 37)*. In addition, just as news of the soldiers' health is important for the audience at home, the brothers desire confirmation of their family's welfare, fearing the loss of loved ones in their absence. Cyrus tells his parents, "It may be you will be afflicted by the loss of more of your children before the war is over or they . . . may loose you without the opportunity of again seeing your faces on earth" *(Letter 66)*. In the case of a death, the family uses letters to express grief and condolences.

"I Wish You Would Write to Me at All Times on Receiving Any Information of Them"

One of the most common news-gathering methods used by the Loves is triangulation, whereby Cyrus, James, and Sam and John (often in camp together) learn of each other's whereabouts and welfare through letters sent from home. Separated into different regiments, the brothers throughout the war depend on letters from home to hear news of each other, as direct contact proves nearly impossible through normal military channels. Cyrus signals such an expectation in his very first letters, closing with an impassioned plea:

> I am at all times anxious to get word from some of you to know how you are getting on and particularly to learn something from S.B. & J.W.L.'s where they are and what they are doing whether they are doing nothing or fighting some and how they are pleased with the place they are at. *(Letter 3)*

In subsequent letters, Cyrus's requests for news become more insistent, such as when he writes, "I would like exceedingly to know something of the boys what they are doing and where they are" *(Letter 13)*. Such concern is characteristic of Cyrus's abiding care: as the eldest brother and first to enlist, he looks out for the welfare of his younger brothers in the service.

Sam and John also express concern for their brothers' welfare. In January 1862, for example, Sam inquires about his brother and uncle: "I hope . . . the next time I hear from you to hear of Cy and Andrews entire recovery from the measles & mumps . . . also I want you to write me . . . how to direct a letter to Cy" *(Letter 20)*. Subsequent letters show that the brothers did endeavor to send letters directly to one another, with intermittent success, but most communication appears to take place through epistles sent from home.The necessity of triangulation is made evident when reading the record as a whole, for the writers frequently make reference to the paucity of communication through official Confederate channels, as when Sam in April 1862 writes, "I have not heard anything of Cy Uncle John or any of our relations" *(Letter 30)*, or John, in October of that year, reports, "We have heard nothing of Cyrus yet he is away up in Ky or Tenn" *(Letter 49)*. Only once does Sam report direct communication with Cyrus, in his letter to his parents dated June 29, 1863: "I received a letter from Cyrus it was written about the first of May. . . . he was in remarkably good health" *(Letter 69)*.

"But I Think It Is My Duty to Write and Risk the Desperate Chances"

Not only do letters share news and the health of the senders, but the act of composition also benefits the writer. Even if the soldier knows that no one else may read his letter, the act of writing allows him to alleviate his anxieties. In his work *Language as Symbolic Action*, Kenneth Burke asserts that one does not need an external audience in order to produce rhetorical acts. He claims that a writer can become his or her own audience, as there are "ways in which we spontaneously, intuitively, even consciously persuade ourselves" (1966, 301). While readers will recognize the importance of the historical information found within the letters, interestingly, the brothers Love often feel as though there is "nothing of importance to write," a phrase that becomes almost a mantra throughout the collection. Their fear that the news they bear will be old by the time the letters reach the family, not to mention their concern that the letters may never reach their relatives at all, raises an interesting question—why bother to write? Yet they continue to faithfully write home whenever an opportunity allows. Beyond reporting and seeking news, the soldiers' reasons for writing include varied personal motivations; the letters here affirm the Confederates' cause, provide catharsis, and— importantly— provide proof of life.

While modern readers know the outcome of the Civil War, the soldiers depict a different version of events, maintaining that the Confederacy will ultimately prevail. In a letter dated November 10, 1861, Cyrus tells his parents "We are now ready for any thing that can come against us and the Almighty being with us we will whip any things that does come" *(Letter 11)*. The following year, on April 28, he repeats, "I feel confident we will whip them badly" *(Letter 31)*. While he uses this phrase less frequently as time passes, he never states he believes the Confederacy will be defeated, only that the war may last longer than previously thought. His words serve a dual purpose: to convince both his relatives and himself that the war will have the desired outcome, and to reaffirm that he, his friends, and his relatives have pursued a worthy cause sanctioned by God. The repetition of these words and phrases wills them to be true, no matter the reality. It is important for the writers to see the words in print regardless of whether anyone else is privy to them: the words help calm and strengthen the men who write them.

Even if the letter contains "nothing of importance," as the brothers often state, the volume of their writing seems to contradict such declarations and suggests that the act of writing was cathartic. The brothers often mention that they have "nothing important left to say" or that they must "close a letter," but then continue to write three or four lengthy paragraphs. The letters also frequently include postscripts. In her work *To Marry an Indian*, Theresa Strouth Gaul explains letters often "resist the closure of the sign-off through the layering of postscripts," suggesting that the writer is enjoying—or otherwise benefitting from—the act of writing (2005, 24).

Even if they truly believe their words are inconsequential, the brothers realize that sending a letter is important for maintaining their filial relationships. Janet Altman, author of *Epistolarity: Approaches to a Form*, explains, "As an instrument of communication between sender and receiver, the letter straddles the gulf between presence and absence; the two persons who meet through the letter are neither totally separated nor totally united. The letter lies halfway between the possibility of total communication and the risk of no communication at all" (1982, 43). Cyrus concedes, "I expect you know the war news from every where better than I can tell you—you cannot get any word to me but I will let you know where I am and how I am getting along evry opportunity" *(Letter 39)*. Even an exchange of banal information is a link: the soldiers knew that a letter reaching home proves that the writer was, at the time of it's posting, still alive.

"Don't Tell the Old Lady How We are Faring It May Trouble Her"

After deciding to write, the soldier must decide to whom he will write. While several recipients exist within the collection, the most common recipients are the Love parents, James Marshal and Terrisa Adeline

Love, and two of the Love sisters, Eliza Terrisa Love (Tea) and Mary Elizabeth Karner (Bettie or Betty). The choice to single out these recipients over other possibilities is worth examining, as it indicates who the men felt could be trusted to circulate the letters and who they felt was most suited to handle certain information. The recipients are mostly women, giving them a prominent role in the family communication network: writing to the soldiers as well as copying or forwarding incoming messages to other members of the family. In essence, the Love women keep lines of communication open.

Sam's decision to primarily write to Tea over his male relatives such as his father or brother Robert reflects his knowledge of the cultural practices of the day. Nan Johnson, author of *Gender and Rhetorical Space in American Life, 1866-1910*, notes the popular opinion of the era: "A woman has correspondence obligations to her home and family no matter where she is, in the home or out, and in whichever the case, her letters are always ministering to the well-being of those at home" (2002, 92).[2] Addressing his letters to his sister is also a mark of respect for her position within the family unit. Both men and women were taught that a man's rhetorical power lay outside the home, but that a woman's rhetorical power or epistolary influence was "defined in familial terms and bounded by the walls of the homes they occupied" (Johnson 2002, 81). Readers can infer Sam's meaning when he tells his parents, "I have generally wrote to Tea because it is more convenint for her than it is for you" *(Letter 41)*. Later he tells Tea directly that when writing his father he "cannot conveniently send a message of love or respect in his letters to the girls" (*Letter 70*). He intimates that he cannot be certain whether his father would undertake to forward the letters in the manner that his sister would, and sends her a separate letter for the sole purpose of ensuring all his female relatives receive well-wishes from him. Sam encounters a problem when addressing a majority of his letters to Tea, however, because Tea is not his only sister. His decision to single Tea out by name in the salutation of the letter apparently causes some jealousy among the Love women, but Sam makes it clear he intends his letters to be read by multiple people, and in Letter 20 he explains to his other sister, Bettie, why he is usually only able to write one letter.

Authors tailor the content of their letters to meet individual recipients' needs. This is demonstrated in an early letter wherein Sam tells Bettie that certain aspects of a recent battle would not interest her, yet he mentions that he would elaborate on these details to Tea in a separate letter. Perhaps deeming the news of little interest to Bettie is really his way of sparing her feelings; Sam may believe that Tea can handle descriptions of the battles but Bettie cannot. The omission can be interpreted, then, as a way to silence the unpleasantness of the war. Gerber notes the common practice of misdirection or omission in correspondence: "To speak in terms of negotiations and ethical discourse might seem, on the face of it, to imply openness, honesty, and forthright dealing. Yet not everything that appears in letters is truthful, and not everything that might be said is committed to paper" (2006, 96). When reading the Love family letters, one notices how frequently Gerber's analysis rings true. For example, even when Sam or Cyrus do talk about battles, they do so in a very routine way, noting when and where the conflicts took place as well as how many soldiers were captured or killed on both sides. The correspondence is what Gerber would define as descriptive rather than expressive (2006, 117). Rarely do Sam and Cyrus discuss the emotional toll of a fight or the manner in which specific people died or how that death affected them personally.

When bad news is presented, it is often coupled with a reaffirmation of the author's belief in the cause and the Deity, so that it appears the brothers are in good spirits. For example, accompanied by the news that the Confederate army is losing men to desertion, Sam writes to Tea, "Everything looks very gloomy at present though I have full faith in the

Justice of our cause that makes me think that we will come out all right yet" *(Letter 68)*.

There is a shift in tone, however, when the recipient is not a relative. James Love, writing in January of 1863 to his friend Dick, presumably a hired man or close family friend of the Loves, delivers an unvarnished glimpse into the life of a soldier: "We are having a rough time of it here it has rained or snowed all the time I have not been in a fight yet nor do I want to be." Although Ellen apparently saw the letter, James warns his friend against spreading the word further: "We have poor beef and bread with a little sugar after this is said all is said oh for such times as we have seen together . . . Dont tell the old Lady how we are faring it may trouble her" *(Letter 58)*. Although this is one of but few extant letters from James, his request that information be withheld from his mother is indicative of the careful way the Love soldiers communicated with their families.

"Tell Robert to Stay at Home Until He Is of Age & Then Encourage Him to Think Closely Before He Joins the Service Atall"

Perhaps the best example of omission can be found in the dual message that the brothers send about the war in general. Though they maintain the Confederacy is sure to emerge victorious, they cannot help but betray feelings of dread or doubt when they discourage their younger brother, Robert, from entering the war. They seem to be torn between the notions of honor and glory attached to service in the war and protectiveness toward their kin. Thus, the tension between a soldier's duty and a brother's duty becomes clear. As the war drags on, the brothers wrestle with the question of whether Robert, the Loves' youngest male child, should be allowed to enlist in the Confederate army, a topic they attend to with some frequency and concern. Robert's older brothers usually caution him on account of his youth. One of Sam's letters, written a year into the war, addresses Robert in passing: "I would be glad if he could come with some clothing . . . but he is too young to go into the war" *(Letter 48)*. Cyrus in March of 1863 sends a letter directly to Robert, possibly at the urging of his parents, who may have desired some support in bridling their youngest son. In 1864, Sam pleads with Tea to "by all means tell Robt to stay at home until fall . . . for I will repeat what I have already wrote to him that the service is something he knows nothing atall about & it does seem to me that he ought to have confidence enough in me to take my advice" *(Letter 79)*. His words intimate that he has omitted some of the worst aspects of the war from his letters; rather than explain the dismal reality, he merely asks Robert to trust him. Cyrus expresses concern about the number of Love sons already in the war, and likely took comfort in having at least one brother at home.

While the Love brothers initially attempt to keep Robert from joining the battle, as the calendar turns, and Robert approaches conscription age, Cyrus and Sam alter their strategy from preventing his coming to ensuring that he joins the proper regiment. A letter from Sam in April of 1864 contains the following concession:

> Tell Robert to stay at home until he is of age & then come to me before he joins the service atall and I will get him in a company of scouts commanded by Capt. Sam Henderson brother of Wm. Henderson of Corsicana and by all means tell him not to join the company that Cobb will be trying to make up. *(Letter 77)*

Taken together, the brothers' effort to dictate Robert's conduct shows the persuasiveness of letters. The combined efforts of Cyrus, Sam, and James, backed by their experience in war, contributed to keeping Robert out of harm's way until the last year of the war.

"I Was Not Aware That You Had Made So Good a Degree of Progress in the Knowledge of Words, the Use of the Pen, and the Correct Use of Language"

While the contents of any given letter in this collection may differ from others, by and large the Love brothers followed a popular blueprint in their composition, cleaving to the expected model while adding a personal touch at crucial junctures. Through the first century of US existence, letter-writing guides were widely circulated and taught to people of all ages. Hugh Blair's work *Lectures on Rhetoric and Belles Lettres* (1783) was the most influential letter guide for school-age children and beyond. In later years, other manuals rose to prominence, including *The Fashionable American Letter Writer* (1837) and Chesterfield's *Letter Writer and Complete Book of Etiquette* (1857). According to popular sentiment, letter writing was an important rhetorical skill that could be practiced and perfected; like penmanship, the closer the produced writing hewed to the ideal model, the more perfect the letter was considered to be. Chesterfield defined letter writing as "an art of conversation on paper," and promoted letter writing as "the skill of adapting a few formal and stylistic rules to particular occasions defined generically as the business letter, the friendly letter, family correspondence, letter of condolence, courtship and marriage, and love letters" (quoted in Johnson 2002, 86). As Johnson explains, "Letter-writing literature promoted the skill of letter writing as indispensable to anyone hoping to achieve social or professional success" (2002, 79). The level of skill one exhibited was often considered a mark of status and class.

Such manuals were most likely read by the Love children during the course of their formal and informal educations; throughout the collection, one notices that the letters often follow a similar structure or style: starting and ending with a salutation, providing exigency, discussing important news, and closing with well-wishes and a signature. By form and habit, the Love soldiers begin each letter by disclosing the occasion which prompted its writing. In short order, the letters relate the health and welfare not only of the sender, but also of those in proximity, assuredly the foremost concern among audiences at home. On occasion when bad health is present, its severity is characteristically downplayed, as in a letter sent by Cyrus from Hopskinsville admitting that "there has been a good deal of sickness in our Regmt but nothing like as bad as it has been in some other Regmts from Mississippi" *(Letter 3)*. Failure to indicate good health could be interpreted as evidence to the contrary—when Cyrus is gravely wounded in the Spring of 1862, he sends no letter for an entire month while convalescing.

Letter writers generally proceed to a description of recent troop movements and battles. The first few months of the soldiers' letters are marked by boredom and anxiety, brashness and despair. As Cyrus confides, "The Regiment are very desirous of a fight before the war ends" *(Letter 10)*. In Letter 20, dated January 1862, Sam gives his sister a short description of his first combat experience. After so long waiting for the fateful day, the troops had grown used to the cry "wolf!" and, as Sam explains, sat "laughing at the idea of getting into a battle for just as we commenced eating the order was given to cap our guns." Soon thereafter battle did arrive.

As the war continues, however, the tone changes, and battle accounts seem to be delivered more out of obligation than from excitement. Cyrus writes, "I am heartily sick of such slaughter a battlefield is a horrid looking sight and I want to see no more of them" *(Letter 59)*. One of the final letters in the collection is little more than a hurried transcript of a battle, as if Sam wishes to dispense with the expected war news as soon as possible before moving onto personal and practical matters.

Chief among those practical concerns are frequent requests for supplies. As the Union blockade tightened, shipments from home were often the only way soldiers could get many necessities. There are requests for jackets, boots, and other clothing in advance of a Northern winter for which the Texans were unequipped. Beyond the soldiers' practical requests, John, like a homesick teenager, wishes for impossible deliveries of homegrown foodstuffs: "All that I write for now is that I want something to eat I wish you would send me some butter a dozen or so of eggs. tie about a peck of sweet milk up in a rag a hat full of Sausages when you kill hogs" *(Letter 14)*.

After the main business of the letter is conducted, the soldiers typically proceed to relate tidbits of military news from fronts near and far, striving to paint a general picture of the war for their recipients at home. Each writer recognizes, however, that his information is unreliable—incomplete at best and erroneous at worst. There was a paucity of legitimate and trustworthy intelligence. Outside of events witnessed firsthand, the soldiers depended upon two unreliable sources: reports from official military channels and news gathered from partisan civilian newspapers.

"The Impious, Contemptible, and Lying sheet at Nashville"

The advent of the Civil War aroused the nation's hunger for daily newspapers, as citizens and soldiers alike strove to learn war news and discover the fates of loved ones. The Love soldiers often suggest newspapers are a faster method of receiving news than the postal service. Newspaper accounts played a part in the Loves' communication, but their veracity was a matter of frequent speculation. In Letter 16, Cyrus expresses his distrust: the "paper states that Price is moving toward Kansas where the same report says he intends making his future operations but I do not believe this at all." On another occasion, Cyrus learns to be skeptical of both the trustworthiness of Northern papers and the clairvoyance of his generals: "Genl Wharton has been reading the Northern papers and has come to the conclusion to bet five hundred Dollars we will have peace in two or three Months" *(Letter 54).*

"None of Us Are Down in the Mouth"

Near the conclusion of a letter, the author typically sees fit to offer a general pronouncement on the state of the war and the high morale among soldiers in camp. Given the reality of the war's progress, this effort may be interpreted as more performative than informative, intended both to mask the army's deficiencies and to comfort the women and men at home, as well as the person writing the letter. The prospect of death lurks in the subtext, especially in Cyrus's letters, but it is scarcely mentioned as an eventuality, so intent are the writers on forecasting a quick and successful ending to the war.

The Loves typically offer sentiments and well-wishes to conclude their epistles, as was expedient and deemed proper by letter-writing manuals. These parting thoughts extend not only to the particular audience to whom the letter is addressed, but also to those who had no doubt gathered to hear the letter read aloud: "We are all well and I do sincerely hope that these few lines will find you all enjoying the same blessing. Give my love to all enquiring friends and more espetially to the family and relations" *(Letter 30).*

"Having a Good Chance With a Good Pen and Ink and Tolerable Paper I Write Again"

After deciding upon whom to write and the letter's topics, soldiers confronted the question of how, exactly, one should communicate a chosen message to a chosen audience. A pragmatic task was procuring letter-writing materials, such as paper, pen, and ink, which were scarce due to war shortages and the Union blockade. Studying the materiality of the Love letters reveals the Loves were an affluent family both in wealth and education, a status that no doubt aided their efforts in composition.

The majority of the letters are in very good condition, legibly written with few tears, holes, or stains on the page. Most are written in black or blue ink with few ink spots or smears, which suggests they took particular care in composition. Beyond the brothers' strong vocabulary and nice penmanship (with the exception of John), the materiality of the letters suggests that the authors were not worried about the cost of paper, as their writing, with a few exceptions, was rarely cramped or small. In "American Civil War Postage Due: North and South," Harry K. Charles explains, "The wartime shortage of paper had a major impact on the ability of an individual to write and then send a letter" (2012, 15). Faced with this shortage, many soldiers resorted to using alternate forms of paper or even turning envelopes inside out; writing as small as possible or using the margins to squeeze in a thought were common practice as well. Though there are some letters within the collection that contain marginal notes (such as Sam's discussion of Sam Houston in Letter 69), these were not customary; the fact that the writers frequently left a fair portion of their paper blank suggests that the Loves, at least in the earlier years of the war, had access to—and could afford—good writing supplies.

"I Have Concluded to Write Again Not Knowing Whether It Will Reach You"

Once the soldiers' letter writing was completed, all that remained was to see that the letters made their way home, no light matter given the distance, and especially as regular Confederate postal lines were compromised as the war deteriorated. Sam seems to have despaired of delivery in April 1862, as he writes, "There is not any news that I could write that you would not hear before you would get this. In fact I doubt very much about this ever getting to you" *(Letter 30).* While this prediction was evidently wrong, his apparent frustration suggests there must have been several preceding letters that did not make it home. As the extant collection only includes those delivered and preserved, there is no telling how many missives were intercepted, miscarried, or otherwise failed to reach their destination.

The letters that do arrive at home often include complaints about the postal delivery system. In one of the first surviving letters from John and Sam (sent by the bearer Mr. Sharp), Sam takes care "to let you know that I had not received a letter from any of you the reason I cannot tell" *(Letter 14).* Cyrus complains that it is not an overall lack of mail arriving to their camp, but curiously a dearth for him specifically: "Many others however are getting letters all the time. . . . Some have had as many as 6 or 8 letters from about in Freestone and Limestone" *(Letter 12).* As time passes, the brothers' complaints become fewer. That this is due to better mail service is unlikely, as it is hard to imagine that the efficiency of the Confederate postal infrastructure improved as the Union army gained control of the Mississippi River and advanced into Southern territory. If the time frame in Cyrus's letters can be accepted as typical, it took nearly three weeks for a letter sent from home to reach the soldiers in camp, and, as can be surmised from Letter 65, nearly six weeks for one to traverse between camps. Such a lengthy delay would have been quite disappointing for writers used to weekly correspondence between Fairfield and Waco. Perhaps explanations from home were enough to placate the men at the front. Or perhaps as the war progressed, the brothers became accustomed to the inefficiency of the postal system, which supports Decker's claim that "letter writers who lack reliable post service learn to make allowance for mischance; they proceed in the assumption that letters are answered as they get through and consent to write five letters on the chance that one might reach the addressee" (1998, 58).

From its outset the Confederacy was aware of the need for a strong postal service, and created its own under the direction of John Henninger Reagan, a Texan like the Love brothers who was appointed by Jefferson Davis as Confederate postmaster general. The degree of Reagan's success was largely a result of his foresight: shortly after attaining his appointment, he solicited the aid of men formerly employed in the Federal postal service, many of whom enlisted and brought with them their account books and records to the Confederacy.

Though by many accounts Reagan did a good job orchestrating the new Confederate system, there were persistent problems. According to Charles Deaton, author of *The Great Texas Stamp Collection,* "The Confederate postal authorities were unable to keep stamps readily available, making it more difficult for Texans to send their mail" (2012, xi), which might explain why the Loves at home had an increasingly difficult time sending word to their sons and brothers. In his article, "Administrative Problems of the Confederate Post Office Department," L. R. Garrison explains that new Confederate stamps were not worth as much as Federal stamps, possibly due to inflation. Moreover, "No authority was conferred officially on the postmasters to issue stamps. Such stamps as were issued by them was done on their own responsibility" (1915, 119-120). As a result, stamps from certain states were worth more than stamps from others. According to Garrison, "In the middle of 1862, [there were] frequent warnings to Texas postmasters that their own stamps would not send a letter 'a mile beyond the Mississippi'" (1915, 120). Since the Love family lived in Limestone County near Waco, Texas, and the Love brothers were most often stationed in Mississippi, Tennessee, and Kentucky, it is likely that Texas stamps were a hindrance to successful delivery. The Loves would have been unaccustomed to such difficulties in sending mail, as prior to 1861, "Post offices were widespread in Texas and a 3-cent stamp would carry a letter up to 3,000 miles, which for a Texan was just about anywhere in the country" (Deaton 2012, 2). Another difficulty in paying postage was uncertainty about how far the letter would need to travel. Even if a letter gave specific instruction about where to direct a response, as most in this collection do, there was no way of knowing if the men would still be at the provided address by the time the instructions were received and a response sent. As a consequence, insufficient postage may have prevented letters sent by the family from reaching the boys.

Cyrus raises other important questions about the mail delivery system in a letter to Tea, wherein he criticizes her use of a long envelope and warns her to seal her letters properly: "I mean the one in the long envelope which was unsealed when it came to hand and did not have the appearance of having been sealed atall you should be careful to seal your letters if you do not wish them to be read by others than those you write to in your last" *(Letter 19)*. Later, Cyrus's warning becomes more direct as he tells his parents, "It is possibly best for you not to undertake to answer as yet there is no certainty that the place to which your letters might be directed would be in the hands of the enemy" *(Letter 31)*.

Many letters in this volume contain information regarding troop movements and battle strategies; if this information fell into the wrong hands, enemy forces could use it to their advantage.

Garrison notes another possible reason for the slow delivery of mail, explaining that the military often got in the way of mail carriers en route: "From the beginning of the war the regularity of the mails had been interfered with because the war department and army officers frequently directed military schedules to be run by the roads in conflict with the schedules of the post office department" (1915, 126). Beyond these temporary delays, some of these mailmen were arrested or detained and thus prevented from delivering the mail on time. In one startling account, the postmaster at Richmond reported "an armed force on March 16, 1862, had surrounded the post office for a time preventing all mail from leaving" (Garrison 1915, 125). Still, the mere fact that letters written by the Love brothers managed to make it home is ample evidence that the Confederate postal service did work, however sporadically.

Faced with mounting difficulties, the Loves increasingly turned to an alternate form of delivery—bearers. Although infrequently available, bearers were a more reliable method of delivery, and could be counted on not only to convey letters to the Love family back home, but also to transport items and letters when the bearer returned. Bearers often emerged unexpectedly: a lucky soldier set to return home on furlough, a man sent back to raise a regiment or gather supplies, or even a soldier discharged for medical or military reasons.

"I am Looking for Brother Every Day. If He Can Only Live to Get Home"

Three letters in this collection *(Letters 5, 53, and 82)* are evidence of another system of communication outside the parameters of correspondence to and from Confederate camps: letters between women in the family. The women's letters provide a glimpse of the home life of Southern women around the time of the Civil War, a significant juncture in epistolary studies. While men and women were often taught to approach writing letters differently, the war caused a shift in gendered expectations of the genre. Prior to and after the war, men were taught to utilize letter writing for business engagements, whereas women were in charge of maintaining domestic correspondence (Johnson 2002, 80).

Out of necessity, men were tasked with helping to maintain family correspondence during the war. A soldier's wife could not, for example, write about her husband's well-being without first hearing from her husband. The war created a need for women and men to take on both roles of correspondence: women had to learn to maintain business correspondence, while men had to learn to negotiate family correspondence. As seen in the Love family letters, Cyrus, Sam, John, and James were up to the task, but not without a few struggles in navigating the politics of family life, such as whom to address on the envelope and within the letter. The women also faced challenges. In the absence of men, women were expected to carry on with family life and attend to business. Fannie's 1862 letter to her mother illustrates the tasks she must manage, including sewing clothes for the children, nursing the sick, and managing the household. Readers learn that sickness was prevalent at home as it was on the battlefield, as Fannie explains she has had a bout of the measles, and seeks her mother's advice about how to cure her ailments *(Letter 53)*. Kimberly Harrison, author of *The Rhetoric of Rebel Women,* explains that Southern women often felt themselves a part of the war. The Love women contributed by sewing clothes for soldiers or gathering supplies, as is mentioned in Fannie's letter.

With four of their five living brothers enlisted in the war, it is not hard to imagine the agony and anxiety of those remaining at home, wondering if their brothers, cousins, sons, or uncles would make it out alive. Though they mention the war in passing, the women's letters in this collection primarily focus on the seemingly mundane tasks of everyday life, such as going to school, doing the laundry, and courting young men. While this might seem irrelevant and insignificant compared to information arriving from the battlefields, this domestic language may be a conscious attempt to instill a sense of normalcy during a time of chaos, to provide reassurance that all is well on the home front. This outlook was in line with popular sentiment; in 1862 the ladies' journal *Southern*

Illustrated News published articles titled "No Gloom at Home" and "The Wife," which encouraged women to be "positive powers of delight" and maintain a sunny disposition (quoted in Harrison 2013, 63). At least in the preserved collection, the women rarely mention the war in their correspondence with one another.

Nancy Gorden Braden Farnsworth

Perhaps most importantly, without the Love women, these letters might not have been preserved for posterity. Scrapbooks containing letters, photographs, and newspaper clippings increased in popularity during the Civil War. Garvey explains that scrapbook manuals were also in circulation during this period; just as letter-writing manuals prescribed gender roles for the task of composition, so too did scrapbook guides. Evidence from the collection suggests that a female relative, perhaps Tea, may have been tasked with the collection of familial artifacts, as she had already been tasked with copying the letters from the boys and sending those copies to others. Sam writes, "Tea coppy this and Send it to bett

Betty for I haven't time to write to her in a different letter and tell her to give my love to all the friends" *(Letter 24)*. Though the extant letters are not contained within a scrapbook, they were preserved with other documents like poems, song lyrics, and newspaper clippings, items typical of the scrapbook genre, another clue to the gender of the collector. It is likely that what we know of the Loves is due to the diligence of the Love women.

"For My Greatest Pleasure Is in Receiving and Reading Letters"

The completion of the circuit—from soldier to sibling or parent, among family and community members, and back to soldier—was the ultimate goal of the communication network established by the Loves. Yet, as readers can glean from the letters, completing a successful circuit was challenging. Even when successful, a full circuit could take several months to complete, and the time lapse in between the composition and delivery of a letter often meant a delay of important information on both fronts, as when both Cyrus and Sam comment upon the deaths of Harriet and Ellen well after the fact.

Despite such delays, the soldiers did receive mail from several relations throughout their time in the war. In a later letter, William Blaine told Bettie, "The memory of loved ones at home has a place in our hearts & especially we boys who think of the young ladies we left behind" *(Letter 71)*. The words of these women and the memories they evoked revitalized the soldiers' dreams of uniting with loved ones when the war was over. The knowledge that family, friends, and home awaited soldiers helped to keep the men focused on their cause. Beyond the information they carried, the letters were physical talismans of home. Every received letter was a visit from a relative or loved one, a means of keeping connected despite the distance, tumult, and violence that conspired to keep them apart.

1. All information pertaining to family history was obtained through a combination of primary accounts from historical records, military databases, Jennifer Mansfield's article "Yours Fraternally Until Death," and living relatives of the Loves: Louise Burton and Maureen Pierce.

2. See Lorri Glover's *Southern Sons* for more information about gendered expectations, including letter writing, in the antebellum South.

Prologue

IN THE MORNING when he wakes; over his noontime meal; with the heat of battle still clinging to his form; at the end of an exhausting march; before he retires to his tent; the soldier arms himself with paper and pen:

I write here by the light of a green Red Oak fire, the fire part having been very necessary.... There is nothing of importance going on about this army. ... I am heartily sick of such slaughter a battlefield is a horrid looking sight and I want to see no more of them.... I am trying to conduct myself as near right as Possible I have not learned to Swear nor drink As there is not three men in camp but what does Both.... All that I write for now is that I want something to eat.... The Almighty has protected me through all the dangers that have surrounded me during the war and I hope will still continue to protect me.... I have had to write in great haste and I will now have to close. We are in good health and Spirits and hope these few hastily written lines may find you and all the friends enjoying the same God's blessing... I would like very much to have some word from you.... Yours In Filial Regard

With the breakfast table cleared; as she sits to sew clothes; after chores are done; once the children are bathed and to bed; a woman picks up her paper and pen:

I am so rusty that it is an exceedingly irksome task for me to write now. It was once the only pleasure I ever really felt, but age is creeping over me now and with it comes stiff joints, scattered thoughts, and a restlessness that will hardly admit of my being still long enough to write, or rather to collect my wandering thoughts. . . . Everything is dull, and everybody are something on the same order. . . . You ought to see the trouble I have in trying to make Josie wear his shoes it has been raining all day and I think if I have dried his shoes and stockins once I have a dozen times Mother I get so impatient some days that I am nearly crazy. . . . I am very anxious to hear from you all. the latest news from the boys and how you are all getting on. . . . I am looking for Brother every day. if he can only live to get home Give my love to all the family

Once in the mail the letters depart to their intended recipients, crossing river and road, hill and valley, until weeks or months later they reach their destination and are at last opened and alive.

The Letters

The first two letters in the collection are written before the start of the Civil War. The first is from Cyrus, the oldest living Love son, who was twenty-nine years old in 1859, to Robert, the youngest, who was twelve at the time. Cyrus wrote this letter from Fairfield, where he was teaching. Fairfield, the county seat of Freestone County, is approximately sixty-five miles east of Waco and twenty-five miles east of Tehuacana, where the Love family lived. This letter is one of two letters addressed specifically to Robert within the collection. The author of the second letter is unclear because the signature is difficult to read, but it may have been written by John Karner, who was married to Mary Elizabeth Love (also called Bettie or Betty throughout the collection). Cyrus mentions his brother-in-law in Letter 1. Together, Cyrus and John Karner were developing a male and female school in Fairfield, and both taught there.

Letter 1

Fairfield
Oct. 30th 1859
Robt M Love

Dear brother:

I received your letter of the 20th Inst[1] which gave me great pleasure and a considerable surprise as I was not aware that you had made so good a degree of progress in the knowledge of words the use of the pen and the correct use of language — It is a great pleasure to me to learn through a letter from you such use of your time in the improvement of your mind

Cousin William Terry Farnsworth served in the 13th Regiment, Tennessee Infantry. The children of Terrisa Adeline Love's sister Nancy, the Farnsworths remained in close contact with their Love cousins.

— I hope you will make use of all your spare time for the improvement of your mind our first duty is to do that which is right towards our Creator and our fellow beings and the next duty is the improvemet of the mind in the knowledge of the arts and sciences so that we may be able to render the labor we have to perform for the support of ourselves and the ability to help others easy and pleasant

I was glad to learn as I did from your letter that you were all in good health — It seems to me that you are rather late in collecting your beeves if you intend driving to the New Orleans market if you aimed to collect many beeves after the date of your letter you will hardly be able to get away from home until several days of Nov are gone which will cause you to be as late as the first of Dec. getting them into market[2]

This letter leaves all the relatives here in good health — Mr Karner is over at Mr Skrugg's he hired several negroes and went over for the purpose of making a tank and some other improvements on his stock farm

— Mr Karner and Mr Jos Philpott purchased some seventy or eighty head of brood mares not long back — they with several other gentlemen conjointly have Purchased the Flying Dutchman[3] and are now keeping him at Avant Parairie

I hope if you go to school that you will a good use of your time by keeping out of bad company, studying hard and learning all you can — our schools are doing very well — ther is are seventy or eighty scholars in the female school and thirty-five or forty in the male school

Our District Court[4] comes on here next week Tell mother that I got a letter from Jas Anderson a short time back he stated that they were all together in Arkansas except Narcissa Edwards and her family that they had suffered greatly of late years but were now doing as well as could be expected under the circumstances I received a letter not long back from Hamilton Farnsworth[5] the relatives were well in Tennessee at that time Hamilton thought it more than likely that his father would come to Texas before long — I write you this short letter Robert by candle light with a bad pen so you could not expect it well done

I would be glad to receive letters from you often and will answer them as soon as I can after getting them

Happiness and good fortune to you and the balance of the family

Truly your brother, C.W. Love

1. Of this month.

2. On average, a herd could maintain a healthy weight moving about fifteen miles per day. Cyrus's estimate is accurate, then, as a trip of 436 miles (from Waco to New Orleans) at this pace would take thirty days.

3. From the context, a prized stallion.

4. The United States District Court for the Western District of Texas, established on February 21, 1857, and presided over by Judge Thomas H. DuVal, one of only two US judges not to resign his post in states that seceded.

5. The Farnsworths were cousins to the Loves on Terrisa Adeline Love's side of the family.

Letter 2

Dallas Texas
Jany 18/60
Dr. J. F. [Morgan]

Dr Sir

I have just arrived in Dallas[1] at my Fathers House where I was happy to meet [Father] and [family]. I have not seated myself for the purpose of writing you a [very] interesting letter as I have not seen enough of Texas even to satisfy myself consequently cannot give you such a description as will correspond [probably] with what I will yet see I must acknowledge so, for I have been disappointed in the general [appearance] of Texas some how or some how else I had fancied that it was a Romantic [fast] looking county but if you have ever travelled from Felicianna to Mayfield[2] you have seen a county that resembles the greater portion of Texas which I have travelled through. It was all an old [time] hard looking country until I got to this (Dallas Co) The timber ranging from 10 to 40 feet high the greater portion of which is post oak, and Blk [oak] though I have seen some fine pine groves and in some creek bottoms good Oak Trees.

The Land generaly is [blk] and sandy the trees on it are low and [scrubby] and look to be a thousand years old Yet it would surprise you to see how the land yields when they [have] season I am told the land, such as I have [described] will yield as if [to] [be]come, ~~and~~ have fine cotton groves and the blk [?] land / but more anon

This (Dallas) is a fine county the best I have seen the greater portion is Prairie and looks grand and magnificent and is rich enough for any purpose I was not pleased with Texas before reaching Dallas but this county will [sorter] do west I am told is better the farmers here have many of them become rich with [labour] by raising stock it is [doubtless] the best stock county known just as far as your eyesight extends you will see the prairie [dotted] with herds of cattle and occasionally sheep they are getting [more] in the spirit of sheep If you moove to Texas bring all your old pots spoons chairs &c & you will need [these] [mind] I tell you I will write again

Give my love to J. H. [Craig] and write to me at Dallas[3]

J. F. [Karner]

1. Founded in 1842, Dallas County had a population of 8,665 at the time of this letter

2. Small towns in southwestern Kentucky separated by twenty miles.

3. This line is written vertically on the left hand side of the page.

Letter 3

Cyrus writes this letter from Camp Alcorn in southwest Kentucky, where the Confederate army was training in preparation for battle. This letter, like many in the collection, is addressed to Eliza Terrisa Love (1844-1908), one of the Love sisters, also known as Tea throughout the collection. In the letter, Cyrus asks for news about three of his brothers: S.B., or Samuel Braden; J. W. L., or John Wilson; and James. As the oldest, Cyrus seems troubled by the fact that all of the Love brothers except the youngest, Robert, had left home to join the war.

Camp Alcorn Hopkinsville Ky.
Sept 1st A.D. 1861
Miss E.T.G. Love :

Dear Sister:

I received a letter from you some time back it was the only one I have had from any one in Texas since I left there. I do not know that you have not written and others may have written also but certain it is no letters get to me while many others have received as many as four or five since we got here=. Uncle A.C.L.[1] came here night before last from Clarkesville where he has been ever since we came there attending to the sick of our Regiment who were left in his charge when we made the forced march to this place Uncle Andrew and myself are well Andrew and Robt High are not entirely well Burgess Modrel has had good health all the time since he started he has not though as I think enjoyed the life of a soldier very much but has been cheerful as far as I know all the time There has been a good deal of sickness in our Reg^{mt} but nothing like as bad as it has been in some other Reg^{mts} from Mississippi= the diseases have been Pneumonia, Measles and Mumps and a good many have died from other Rg^{mts} but few from ours, and none as yet from our company[2] but Melville Clough and Elick Strain at this place and young Robinson of Cotton Gin at Princeton are dangerously sick Clough has been sick nearly ever since we came here[3]= We have had a good deal of rain in the last two weeks and some sleet and snow[4] day before yesturday but no severely cold weather — the weather has been of that changable character calculated to create colds — Our camp life is generally dull and monotonous but is sometimes relieved by exciting preparations for a march and at others by the presence of the ladies of Hopkinsville

I believe I stated in a letter written abut the time we got to this place that Uncle John W Love came down to the Road between Jackson Miss= and Decatur Ala— to see us but did not stay with us long as we did not delay any time in coming through from Memphis to this place if we had remained at Clarksville he said he thought he would come up to see us= if we go into winter Quarters and I can get a furlow I intend going down to see him I have learned throug letters to others that the clothing prepared for our company has been started to us they may get to us and they may not but if they do not we stand a chance to suffer if the winter should be cold as there is but little likely hood that the Government will be able to supply the Soldiers with anything like enough of clothing to keep them comfortable[5] = if the Northern forces do not go into Winter Quarters as they say they will not we may have some hard marches yet this winter but if they are whipped as I think they will be in the three principal fights which I think will be likely to take place soon they will be compelled to go into Winter Qrs to collect and protect the remnant of their forces and peace will most likely be concluded before the campaign opens in the Spring of next year

but these Ideas of peace are no more than conjecture we may be here all of the three years and more.

Kentucky is one of the old countries a great part of it being badly worn but some of it is very good it is a great state for the raising of tobacco if we might judge from the barns full that are seen on the Road

Situated as I am here I can learn but very little of interest things of considerable importance might take place in a short distance of me and you would learn of it before I would— I am at all times anxious to get word from some of you to know how you are getting on and particularly to hear something from S.B. & J.W.L.s where they are and what they are doing whether they are doing nothing or fighting some and how they are pleased with the place they are at. I thought three of us were enough to be out at one time and James should have staid at home and not have gone to galveston[6] = When you write let me know whether father and Uncle David have sold their wool or not and what they got for it — I will write to yo again soon   Your fraternall

C.W. Love

I can now appreciate the rich and endearing blessings of a home peace and plenty and if God will I will enjoy them again but not before the three years are out[7] and possibly not then certainly not then if my services should continue to be needed in the war

Your &c.
C W Love

1. Andrew C. Love, General and Staff AA Surgeon in Cyrus's regiment.

2. In the Confederate army a typical infantry regiment was composed of ten companies, which included about one thousand men led by a colonel, a lieutenant colonel, major, and ten captains (one per company). A company generally consisted of one hundred men with one captain, one first lieutenant, one second lieutenant, one first sergeant, four sergeants, and two corporals.

3. Two out of three Civil War deaths occurred from disease rather than from battle.

4. The mention of snow is curious, given the letter's date.

5. At this time many of the soldiers were clad in irregular uniforms. Cyrus's company, being from Texas, would be unaccustomed to cold winter temperatures.

6. The Texas Second Infantry regiment was organized by J.C. Moore during the summer of 1861 in Galveston. While James possibly enrolled at this time, extant military records indicate his joining Company G of the Twentieth Texas Cavalry in spring 1862.

7. It seems that Cyrus is on a three-year contract, an unusual length for Confederate volunteers at the outset of the war, when the typical term of enlistment was one year. The Confederate Re-enlistment Law of December 11, 1861 stipulated that every soldier who reenlisted for three years or for the duration of the war was promised a bounty of fifty dollars and a sixty-day furlough.

Letter 4

The first letter in the collection from Sam Love finds him encamped in Graves County, Kentucky, at Camp Beauregard, an ill-fated installation that was abandoned by the military in February of 1862—and burned to the ground a month later—because of disease. Fifteen hundred soldiers were killed there, not in combat, but by pneumonia, typhoid fever, and other ravages. Outside of small skirmishes along the Ohio River, up to this point there were few engagements with Union forces in the western theater.

Camp Beauregard Sept The 8 =61
Dear sister I wrote you a few lines the other day but as I had but a very short time to write it I did not write but very little. Almost every one in

Samuel Braden Love (Sam)

camps have been sick within the last week thoug all are about well now=We marched from camp Tarrant on last monday=the line of men in double file was about six hundred yards long the regiment I think will be filled this week though no one knows when or where we will be ordered there is about as many opinions as the is men=however there is a great deal of advantage[1] in us being here for we are learning the Cavalry drill very rapidly=there is a report here that six war steamers have left fortress Monroe[2] with four thousand men on board if so Texas may look out

There is no more news of importance. Pete & I went to see the Misses Fares this evening & enjoyed ourselves finely=they told us that they were going to take Supper with us tomorrow evening they also gave us a potatoe apiece as the did the evening after they supped with us before I like them very mouch for the acquaintance I have with them.

I am intruding on the sleeping hours of a family & I will have to bring this to a close and as I have no other word to send to Nannie give her my love. I hope these few lines will find you all enjoying good health so with these few lines I remain your brother

Sam

P.S Give my love to all the family S.B.L

1. There is an inkblot over this word.

2. A military installation in Hampton, Virginia, at the southern tip of the Virginia Peninsula, which remained in Union control throughout the war.

Letter 5

Because it was undated, this letter was not originally numbered by curators, but we surmise it was written September 12, 1861, and place it here. Assuming that "your friend, Mollie" is the author, it was probably written by Mollie Neal, who is mentioned throughout the collection. It is also possible that Tennessee (Tennie) Love was the author, and that she made the request for a letter on Mollie's behalf, since she mentions "brother John" and requests to have a letter backed, a common practice among the Love siblings.

Bosqueville Texas Sept. 12
Miss. Tea. Love,

Dearest Tea
I have just finished my letter to brother John and will now write to you. We arrived here safe and sound we are all boarding at Mr. [Burgess]. I am verry much pleased with Mr. Collier I think he is an excellent teacher.[1] Tea I do wish you would come up here to see us but I know you will not. Tea Mr. Collier told us to write a letter to him and give them to him next friday we have all got ours written except Nannie[2] who found a novel to read and could not write.

There are three ~~letters~~ girls boarding here Eno young, Minnie [Kuy]kendall, Frannie Daniel. They are very nice girls There are no pretty boys here. I saw Mr Bradcock as we were comeing up here he looked so nice you wish it had been you in the plac of me dont you. We saw another pretty boy in waco. Tea — Lizzie[3] has written to you Nannie is writing they can tell you all that I don't write I have not been here long enough to get acquainted yet so I dont know any thing to write.

Have you seen the captain since we left?

I am so tired. Tea please write me a composition and send it in a letter. Maggie and Lizzie send their love to you.

Write soon to your friend, Mollie

Send this letter to John you do not know what I said about you in my letter it was something good Please back John's letter for me[4]

1. Mr. John C. Collier (1834-1928) was a Cumberland Presbyterian minister who taught at the Waco Female Seminary and later became president of the college. Located in Waco, Texas, the school was formally known as Bosque Academy or Waco Female Seminary. During the Civil War it was also called Bosqueville Male and Female College. It was the first coeducational college in McLennan County. The school was chartered on February 16, 1858.

2. Perhaps a nickname for one of the Farnsworth cousins.

3. Mary Elizabeth's daughter.

4. Written on back in line with vertical fold.

Letter 6

In a month's time, Sam moved from Camp Beauregard to Fort Smith, Arkansas, a distance of over three hundred miles. In the letter, Sam talks about the movement of soldiers between two forts; it was about seventy miles from Fort Smith to Fort Gibson, Oklahoma, which was located in what is now Muskogee County.

Fort Smith Oct the 8th ^1861^

Dear Sister

I embrace the present opportunity of writing you a few short lines to inform you how We are all getting on on.

We are all in tolerable health & in fine spirits. I wrotte you word at McKinney that I would not write you word any more till I reached this place. but I come very near not coming here. After we left McKinney We marched on finely [?][1] till we come to to the forks in the road where one went to Fort Gibson & the other to fort Smith= After we had traveled the Ft= S= road about two miles we met an express[2] from Gen Mcullough ordering us to fort Gibson. We turned back to the F..G.. road & marched on & overtook the first Division that evening.. from there the first & second Divisions marched tog together one day & two days later the whole regiment got together & marched on toward Fort Gibson until within one days travel of the Fort when another express come from Fort Smith to Colonel Stone.. to send 20 men to drive some baggage waggons to camp Jackson= so I volunteered for the purpose of getting to come to this post office= but when I got here I did not ~~fine~~ find a sg single ~~letter~~ letter We are ordered on to the scene of action & there is no telling how soon we may get in to a fight though it is possible we may not get into a fight this fall=if not I dont k know where we will winter at

We have=so far had but little cold weather thoug we are expecting it all the time =& if we have a cold winter there is a great many in the army that will suffer unless we get good winter quaters= The Creek Indians are Dissatisfied & have turned against us. as you wil read all the news I could write you befor this leter would reach you I will end it by sending my love to all the family as well as your self. Give my love to Nannie & all enquiring friends. The next letter I write I intend to send to Father

All the Tiwacany[3] boys are well. I dont know where you will Direct your letters=but you can Direct them to were you think I am am to Colonel Stones regiment Second Regiment Texas cavalry in To the care of Capt. Bridges

Write as soon as you get this for I am anxious to hear from you all—
With these few lines I remain your brother

S..B.. Love

1. Illegible mark, struck through.

2. Telegraph or telegram.

3. Tehuacana, the Loves' hometown. There are variations of the spelling of the town throughout the letters.

Letter 7

Most of Cyrus's letters are addressed to his parents, James Marshall Love and Terrisa Adeline Braden Love. Although his letter of September 1 was posted from Kentucky, Cyrus's mention of Fairfield, Marshall, and crossing the Red River in the following letter makes it clear his company had moved back into Texas in the interim, before moving east once more. Here he writes from Minden, Louisiana, just north of Shreveport and approximately twenty miles east of the Texas border.

At Camp 15 miles East of Minden
Clayborn Parish La.
Oct 14th A.D. 1861
Jas M &T.A. Loves:

Dear parents:

I have been in the land of Cypress Beach[1] and Maple since I crossed Red River. We are to night in 60 or 65 miles of Monroe. We are now to go to Memphis instead of Corinth And it is my belief that we will be ordered from there up into Kentucky— I will however write to you from Monroe and Memphis as soon as I get to those places I have been in good health since I left home. We are all walking some do not stand it so well so far but they are getting better every day. I can walk about as well as the best of them I have not ridden on horse or wagon more than 20 miles since I left Fairfield We all rode on the cars about 18 miles out from Marshal. We have been treated very kindly by all except one man from Fairfield to this place There will be but a small crop of cotton gathered in this state (about such as will be gathered in Texas corn has been good here. Nearly all the young men have gone from this section to the war. We heard from an old man on the road to day that fighting had begun at the mouth of the Mississippi that firing had been heard in that direction for 2 days and that the ballproof vessel called the Gopher[2] had gone out to try its power against the U.S. vessles. You no doubt hear these thing before I do We also heard from the same source I think Galveston had given itself into the hands of the Federal forces without any sort of resistance but we can hardly believe this.[3] We have heard of some severe fighting in Western Virginia between Lee and Rosencrantz the fighting is reported to have lasted two days Rosencrantz having been killed and his army completely routed I have nothing of much importance to write but as we will pass by a post off. tomorrow morning I thought I would drop you a few lines to let you know how we were getting along our relatives in the company and Terry Wylie in the McLellan County company are all in good health and every member of both companies are improving in health.

I wish you would write to me at Memphis direct your letters to the care of Cap[t]. W. L. Moody Co[l] Greggs Regiment[4] be sure if you hear from the boys to let me know what you have learned and let me know where they are gone No more at present

Yours truly till death.
C.W. Love

1. Probably beech (another tree).

2. A flat-bottomed steam ship that belonged to Clarence B. Moore.

3. The Federal blockade of Galveston began on July 2, 1861 with the arrival of USS *South Carolina*, but the town remained in Confederate hands for the next fourteen months.

4. A successful businessman in Texas, William Lewis Moody organized Company G of the Seventh Texas Infantry in 1861 under the command of John Gregg. Moody survived the war, eventually reaching the rank of colonel. Gregg, a Texas judge in 1860, began the war as an elected member of the Confederate Congress, but soon resigned to form the Seventh Texas Cavalry, of which he was colonel. Gregg moved up through the ranks of the Confederate army to become brigadier general before he was killed in battle in northern Virginia in October 1864.

Letter 8

Cyrus's route takes him through Monroe, an important Civil War crossroads in northeastern Louisiana a little over seventy miles from Minden. From there he traveled about 125 miles east to Jackson, Mississippi, then another 200 miles north before crossing the Tennessee state line. The Kentucky battle he refers to may be a skirmish at Barbourville on September 19 that was a Confederate victory, but it engaged far fewer forces, with fewer losses, than Cyrus reports here.

At Camp near Memphis
Oct 20th A.D. 1861
Jas M. & T.A. Loves:

Dear parents:

I wrote to you before arriving at Monroe and have had no opportunity to do so since. We got on the cars at Monroe yesturday at 5 O,Clock—came from there to Vicksburg by 10 Oclock from there to Jackson Miss—by Canton and Grenada to this place. the night we left Monroe it had rained all night and every thing was thoroughly wet by the time we had finished loading. There has nothing transpired worth writing about since I wrote last except what you may possibly learn before this gets to you— it is that there has been a fight in Kentucky reported in which there were said to be about 1500 Confederates against 2000 Federals The Federals getting whipped loosing 70 or 80 and a good quantity of arms and provisions the Confederates loosing but few probably some ten or fifteen. there was a man from New Orleans who came to Memphis this morning on the same train of cars with ourselves who reported that the little vessle called the Gopher would go down and attack the blockading fleet this morning it is the same vessle about which we have heard so much. I was informed this morning by a citizen of Memphis that there were two other boats of the same kind being built at or near the city. I have seen no one that I knew since I left Marshal. I may however have neglected to say in my former letters that Burgess Modrel had joined a company I think the Upsher County Greys Burgess was with us up to the night after we left Shreveport. where our company and Capt Granberry[1] (of McLellan County) left them and came on together to Monroe at this place we left Capt Granberry as one of his men was too sick to travel. I find some men as I pass along through this region of country particularly since we crossed the Mississippi who if they and their Interests were all that was to be defended I for one would do nothing: but leave them to the Mercy of the Yankees. but there not many of this kind on the Road from where we started to Monroe and at the latter place we found one real whole sould fellow who was constantly engaged in supplying us with what was necessary.

This leaves the entire company in good health or nearly so there has been one or two having chills nearly evry day since we left home

Oct 21st 1861

Some of the boys in our mess were tired and Sleepy and wished the bed made down this bothered me then I had to issue rations after night and consequently did not finish writing last night but have nothing of importance since I begun last night

I think the calculation is that we will be here some time but I do not know how long write to me often letters from home at this time will much more gratifying than at any other I will write again as soon as I learn any thing of importance

Yours truly and affectionately till death
C.W. Love

1. Hiram Bronson Granbury led a unit of soldiers from Texas in John Gregg's brigade. He was elected major shortly after this letter was written and was eventually commissioned as a brigadier general. He was killed in action during the Battle of Franklin, Tennessee, in November 1864.

Letter 9

This is one of the few letters in the collection where the address on the outside of the letter has been partially preserved. The envelope is part of the letter, which is contained on one sheet of paper. Though the letter is torn, the reader can make out the words "Springfield Limestone Co. Texas." The letter also contains several mathematical calculations along the outside edges and the bottom of the page, possibly in reference to the number killed in battle or estimations of the possible crop profit Cyrus mentions in the letter. Small diagrams accompany some of the calculations.

The battle at Leesburg, Virginia, that Cyrus mentions in the last paragraph is the Battle of Ball's Bluff. Fought on October 21, it was an infamous defeat for the Union in which scores of Union troops were forced into the Potomac River. Accounts vary, but records show that the Union army lost between 750 and 1000 troops (killed, wounded, captured, or missing), whereas the Confederates lost around 150.

At Camp East of Memphis
Oct. 25th AD. 1861
Ja^{s}M &T.A. Loves:

Dear parents:

This leaves myself and the relatives in camp in good health the two companies that arrived first (ours & the McLellan County Company) are in comparatively good health—five other companies of Greggs Regiment are just now getting in to camp Co^{l} Gregg received day before yesterday an order from the War department to move as soon as possible to a point near the Kentucky line—I think the place to which we will be moved is Clarksville on the Columbia river about fifty miles from Nashville the Co^{l} Telegraphed on yesturday to know whether we would move by companies or wait until the regimen is formed he will know to day so by tomorrow we may be on the march to some other place I will let you know as soon as we get to the place of destination how to direct yur letters and give you any further information that I may have the right to give you I will say just here fearing that I would forget if I delay longer the wool in this section is selling from what I can learn from 8.50 ^cts^ to $1.00 [pr] [lb] I think speculators are buying it up as we were coming out we passed several men we took to be speculators from the way they talked they said they were compelled to have the wool I think they have possibly mad a contract with the government to furnish the troops with clothing but this is a guess only—they said they were compelled to have it because many of the troop were nearly naked troops are going toward Kentucky as fast as possible[1]

When I left home I thought we would be able to buy things we needed here at cheaper rates than elsewhere but things are exactly different Common [Kersey][2] that sold Fairfield for from thirty to fifty cents pr yd is selling here for from .75^cts^ to $1.00— and all other things in proportion excet probably sugar and molasses. beef is 15^cts^ Bacon from .25^cts^ to .30^cts^—The fight at LeesBurg last Monday was a complete rout to the Federals they lost 500 killed 300 drowned in crossing the river and 200 prisoners but our loss was sever 400 killed and 300 wounded & I learn from a Cap[t] Dupree of Co[l] Griers Reg= that McCullough did not do that Regiment justice in his report of the fight at Oak Hill. he says that Griers Regiment was ordered in persuut of the enemy and killed a good many taking five cannon You will possibly learn all these things faster by mail than I could inform you by letters but any thing I know I will write any way you can write to me at any time from where I write my letters to you and they will be forwarded to me at any other place I may have moved to

Yours in affection and filial regard till death
C.W. Love

1. The bottom right corner was torn from the page at the time the letter was written.

2. A type of course woolen cloth.

Letter 10

Camp Alcorn at Hopkinsville Ky.
Nov 6th A.D. 1861
Ja[s]. M. & T.A. Loves:

Dear parents:

I wrote at Memphis but did not have an opportunity to mail the letter and did not send it at-all neither have I had time and opportunity to write since I left there until now and not much of importance to write at this time.

We were hurried through in quick time from Memphis to this place traveling in open Stock Cars most of the time traveling both night and day in this condition sleeping as best we could on the cars living on molasses and bakers bread or hard bread the last of which is nothing more than a thin cake of flour baked hard— I think there have but four or five died since the Regiment left Texas none have died in our company—there are however a good many in the Regiment sick at the present time 3 or 4 in our company the is at least one third of the Regiment that have bad colds but there is hardly a man who woud be kept out of a fight if one should take place we were ordered from Memphis to Clarksville Tenn—We got to Clarksville by Steam boat down the Cumberland in the morning a while after mid night and there was an order came there next day for us to march immediately to this place which we did in pretty quick time over a bad road expecting when we got here to get a fight—but it appears now that there is not much prospect for one to come off very soon unless we go from here to find it and the Regiment are very desirous of a fight before the war ends this post is commanded by Genl. Tilman[1]—I have seen him and his conduct together with his reputation here indicate that he is the right kind of a man= Terrys Reg.[2] is at Boling Green 50 or 60 miles from here one of his companies attacked two companies of the enemy and hardly left one of them to tell the tale (so report has it) and it is generally believed here= the is a strong enough force here now to cause Genl Tilman to feel confident that he will be able to whip any number of the enemy that can come against him Two or three of our company were left at Clarksville sick and Uncle A.C.L was left in charge of them they are getting well and will be here soon—I saw uncle John a short time at Jackson Miss. he and family were well I also saw Walker love and Mary at Memphis they were well the Camp East of this place and about a mile and a half from us has meazles and mumps they will no doubt soon be in our camp but there are not many who have not already had them

Direct your letters to=

C. W. Love
Capt Moody Company
Col. Greggs Reg—
Hopkinsville Ky

Any thing of importance taking place I will let you know it if I am permitted to write

Yours in filial regard until death
C. W. Love
Mr^s^. C.W. J.W. & S.B.Love[3]

1. Lloyd Tilghman from Kentucky had just been promoted to brigadier general in October, 1861. After his capture at Fort Henry and subsequent release, he was killed during the Vicksburg Campaign in 1863.

2. Terry's Regiment, the Eighth Texas Cavalry, was also known as "Terry's Texas Rangers." For more information, see Jeffrey D. Murrah, *None but Texians: A History of Terry's Texas Rangers.*

3. These words are written in pencil rather than pen; the handwriting appears to be similar to the rest of the letters written by Cyrus.

Letter 11

The autumn of 1861 was heartening for the Confederate army, as it won a number of small skirmishes in both the western and eastern theaters. Important among the South's victories was the Battle of Belmont-Columbus on November 6, 1861, which was fought from both sides of the Mississippi River at Belmont, Missouri, and Columbus, Kentucky. Although troops under Ulysses S. Grant destroyed a Confederate camp at Belmont, the Confederates ultimately repulsed Grant's attack on the port city of Columbus, thus maintaining, for a time, the Confederacy's strategic hold on Mississippi River traffic. At this point, the Loves had yet to see battle.

Camp Alcorn Christian County Ky
Nov— 10th A.D. 1861
Ja^s^ M & T.A. Love^s^:

A group of soldiers from the 8th Regiment Texas Cavalry, also famously known as Terry's Texas Rangers.

Dear parents:

I have learned some very cheering news on yesturday a messenger arrived at this place bringing the news that our forces at Columbus had been attacked by the Lincoln army to the number of of about ten thousand land forces on this side the river a strong force on the other bank and seventeen gun boats on the river our forces came out and met those on this side and nearly destroyed the whole of them a man here who is just from there says he could walk on dead bodies a distance of seven miles= the Lincolnites went in to the river rapidly as the only chance for escape the Lincolnites supposed Gen[l] Pillow had left the other bank and I suppose this is the reason why they thought fit to throw forces on the West bank what the result on that side has been I have not ascertained— the guns from the fort soon silenced the gun boats and compelled the enemy to quit them It has been another glorious victory for us

It is reported that that there have been fights at Lees Burgh and Manasses in which we are said to have been successful nothing however confirmatory of either—We are under the command of Gen[l] Lloyd Tilghman who gave us an informal review yesturday he then went from here to town where he found a messenger from Columbus bearing the news of the figh—he immediately returned to the camp to inform us= he seed to me to be the[1] right sort of a man and his talk indicates that he will give us a fight the first favorable opportunity he says we are a fine Regiment— thinks or at least he said we could whip them ten to one=there are said to be 600 men from this county in the Federal army—there are also 600 or 700 Secessionists—there are said to be about 5000 Ky[s] in the Federal army—the Secessionists of the country are the true men of Kentucky—liberal whole souled men We are to day finishing the election of Officers of the Regiment=Gregg is elected Co[l] Clough of Marshal Lieutenant Co[l] and I think Cap[t] Grandberry of the Waco Rifles will be elected Major I heard from Uncle A.C.L. yesturday he was left at Clarksville in charge of the sick of our Company one of whom is not well enough to come forward yet=John, Andrew, Rob[t] High and Burgess Modrell are in good health Geo. Blain is not in good health—Geo Bradley Wm Harris and J[no] A. Womack are not well Geo B is lying in a foot of me now he thinks it exceedingly doubtful whether he will get home again but if he does he says if he does he will one of these Mississippi Rifles they are a fine gun the Regiment are almost entirely armed and equipped= we are now ready for any thing that can come against us and the Almighty being with us we will whip any things that does come I will write again in a few days if I have any thing to write I have had but one letter from home since I left would be glad to get one at any time

Yours in filial regard until death

C.W. Love

P.S. I do not mean by what I said of Mr. Bradley that he is in any danger from ill health=he has the headache bad cold and the bluus a little there are none of the sick in camp that are not improving and all the sickness that is may be said to be from colds

Yours &c
C.W. L

The name of the commander of this post is spelled Tilghman but pronounced as if written=Tilman

1. There is a black ink stain partially obscuring this word.

Letter 12

The envelope that corresponds to this letter has been preserved within the collection and indicates that the letter was sent from "C.W. Love Capt. Moodys Company Co[l] *Gregg*[s] *Reg Tex Vo*[l]*." It is addressed to "Mr. Ja*[s] *M. Love Springfield Limestone Texas." In addition, it contains both a hand stamp and a handwritten note saying "due 10." According to Charles Deaton, author of* The Great Texas Stamp Collection, *Postmaster General John Reagan authorized Confederate postmasters to locally create provisional stamps or resort to manuscript and hand stamped markings until Confederate stamps were issued (2012, 11). This letter's date indicates that new stamps had not yet arrived, making a hand stamp necessary.*

Hopskins-ville Christian Co Ky=
Nov. 21st A.D. 1861
Ja[s] M & T.A. Love[s]:

Dear parents:

This leaves myself and the other Relatives in good health excepting colds— Uncle A.C.L. has not come up with us yet he was at left at Clarksville as we came through there with some 20 of the Regiment that were sick 3 or 4 of them were of our company the last one of our Company will come up in a bout a week one of the number that were left died two or three have died since we came here we left here yesturday was a week ago as we thought to fight the enemy at Madisonville but we were taken to Princeton Caldwell County where we remained a few days but found no enemy in a body= the worst enemy here are the Unionists—the little 6 lb cannon which we had with us went out the day before we left Princeton and returned the day we left they found a gun boat on the Columbia River some where below Canton and shot at it once but fired no more as they concluded they were not able to injure it but they afterward heard that the shot they fired damaged their wheel house some and broke the hog chain the artilery men said the boat got off some distance and fired back at the little cannon with shell Ball and Grape[1] but did no harm we could hear the firing to Princeton Distance about 30 miles there are a good many Texans here and elsewhere in Ky Terry^{s} Regiment is at Boling Green and there are a good many companies in other Regiments. It is about 30 miles to Princeton we left here yesturday was a week ago at sun down traveled till 11. O'Clock slept on our arms and got to Princeton next evening about 4 O'Clock=We left there ^day before^ yesturday about an hour before sun down and got here yesturday about sun down=We have a report here that a fight took place at Pikeville in Missouri[2] in which we are said to have lost about 200 men the enemy are reported to have lost about a thousand in killed and wounded but as I have before said you are more likely to get the truth than we=there is possibly a good deal of skirmishing but no prospect of a general battle

I would be very glad to have some news from you I have had but one letter from home since I left many others however are getting letters all the time some have had as many as 6 or 8 letters from about in Freestone and Limestone We have no news of importance when there is any if I am living I will write immediately and will let you know all that I can=Genl (Tilman) his name is spell'd Tilghman has been sent to Columbus Genl

Clark takes his place here I know nothing as yet about him what there is of this is a considerable scribble I will write again soon

Yours in filial regard till death

[C W L][3]

1. Cyrus is referencing types of ammunition: respectively, a projectile with explosives; a solid spherical projectile made from iron; and large caliber shot contained in a canvas bag.

2. Perhaps the Battle of Ivy Mountain fought near Pikeville, Kentucky on November 8-9, 1861, a Union victory.

3. The page is torn obstructing the signature, but the handwriting, information in the letter, and valediction line are consistent with Cyrus's prior letters.

Letter 13

Camp Alcorn

Hopkinsville Ky—

Nov. 29th A.D. 1861

Jas M. & T.A Loves:

Dear parents:

This leaves me in good health except that I yet have a little cold John W has been smartly afflicted to with cold which affected his throat very much in connection with which he had some fever— he has also had very sore hands he is a good deal better however at this time Robt High and Andrew are complaining some Andrew had a chill yesturday= there are about 30 of our company who were declared not fit for duty Uncle A. C. was left at Clarksville when we left that place and has never come up having been left in charge of the sick boys all of whom are not well yet.=

I think we are on the eve of a move from this place to some other part of the Globe I do not know and can hardly imagine where Some think we will go to Bolin Green. others that will go to Columbus and still others think to Memphis=My Impression however is that the Infantry will be moved some where near Columbus and the Cavalry to Bolin Green this is all mere conjecture however [our stock][1] were moved to Clarksville yesturday and our surplus [camp goods][2] are going that way to day there is a report in camp to day that there was a fight at Bolin Green a few days ago in which we were said to have given the yankees a terrible brushing but the report is not believed Dr. Riddle of the Waco Co is present he says he got a letter from some one in Terry[s] Regiment in which the Regiment is said to have lost about seventy five by disease and that as many more are sick and will likely not be fit for duty this winter

We are made to understand here that the Northern army will not go into Winter Quarters any where else but at Nashville and Memphis. This I guess is another boast like that of Scott[s] intention to have Richmond and Memphis by the 15th of last July[3]

The paper which bears the name of Louisville Courier which was formerly published at Louisville and now at Bolin Green gives in its last issue an account of vast numbers concentrating near or at crab Orchard Ky with the design as is supposed of making a descent on Bolin Green and thence to Nashville large forces are said to be concentrating about Cairo for the purpose of descending by way of Columbus to Memphis Kentucky has by her convention at Russelville seceded from the Old Government and appointed a provisional Government[4] great numbers of the people of this state are unionists but from what I can learn I believe a considerable majority are for secession 64 counties are said to have been represented in the convention they being considerably more than half of the State and a great part of the State not represented on account of the Northern forces having possession of it and it being known that a man dare not exercise the rights of a free man where they have the power=Maryland has a Legislature of Union men on the sam grounds

If we are moved from here I will write you again soon=I would like exceedingly to know something of the boys what they are doing and where they are

I rec^d a letter from Terissa since I left home in answer to one written to you=it was the first and last that I have had from home I hear a little something now and then through some other persons letters from near home but nothing from thince=the Drum has just beat for dress parde and I must quit this letter=It has been raining for several days with some intermissions

I will write again soon write when you think fit

C W Love

1. A water stain on the page obscures these words.

2. A water stain on the page obscures these words.

3. Referring to Winfield Scott's "Anaconda Plan," an early strategy to economically strangle the Confederacy via naval blockade.

4. The ordinance of secession was signed in Kentucky on November 20, 1861, and approved by a convention of two hundred people representing sixty-five counties of the state. Although this group sought admittance to the Confederate States, Kentucky did not formally secede from the union and the state government remained loyal to the United States.

Letter 14

Attached to Sam's letter of December 5, which follows, is John Wilson Love's first extant letter, which he added to the bottom of brother Sam's.

Camp Washington Ark Dec=the 5th 1861

Dear father as Mr. Sharp is going to Start home in the morning I thought I would write you a few lines to let you know how we are getting on & what we have been doing since I wrote my last. I wrote from Camp

Evans on the 15th of last month.. We were then camped near the line of Mo=the next day after I wrot an order come for us to march within two hours to Springfield..We were ready at the allotted time & soon on the march..The fourth day about 10 o'clock we marched into the town..^but^ by^we^ found nobody no was there to oppose us=Gen Mcullough sent out a scouting party to find out what they could about the enemy=Capt=Whites & Capt.. Bridges companies were the scouts so we started without any thing to eat & just as a heavy rain commenced falling & marched very fast till near night & camped next morning we marched 6 or 8 miles & took some union men but turned them loos they told us that we were surrounded by 5 or 6 companies of union & that 4000 men or federal troops were in 10 miles of us & to confirm the report an old man that we ~~knee~~ knew to be a good Southorn man told us the Same & ~~persuaded Capt White to~~ tried to persuade Capt.. White to turn back but he would not do it but turned to the right to see about the 4000 went 6 miles & found that the report was false=we camped at a mr Scotts an unkle of [~~m~~] Capt.. Whites wife & he give us supper and breakfast..next moring early we were on the march for a town by the name of lebanon 55 miles from Spr..=about 2 miles from mr Scott's we over took 12 movng waggons & searched them for guns & found 15 or 16 guns they were moving North..We searched ~~500~~ 50 or 60 waggons during the day & found about 50 guns=We threw them all away but two Minnie rifles[1] & 2 shot guns When we got to Lebanon the citizens of the town give us dinner & we turned back for Spr= & marched about 10 miles & camped..= that night was the second that I stood guard during the scout & about 10 o'clock it commenced raining & rained till 12 & then it commenced blowing from the north & the way it was cold was not a little.. next morning we started on for camps about 4 o'clock= & marched 6 miles to a little town by the name of Jerico.. after we had gone half beyond the town the citizens sent for us to come back & they would get us breakfast so we turned back and got our breakfast.. & started on

John Wilson Love.

our way the wind blowing very cold.. we marched on to Spr.. without molestation. I shall bring this letter to a close as I have not time to write a long one.

My main object in writing this letter is to let you know that we are well all except Jasper Bowden & Frank Sharp also to let you know that I had not received a letter from any of you the reason I cannot tell. Direct your letters to Fort Smith to the care of Captain Ross..Co[l].. Stones Regiment Texas Cavalry

Pa Sam finished his letter I thought I would say a few words partly to let the people of our country together with yourself know that I could write a short letter yet in a few days I will write a general history of our trip & All that I write for now is that I want something to eat I wish you would send me some butter a dozen or so of eggs. tie about a peck of sweet milk up in a rag a hat full of sausages when you kill hogs Pa I never hooked[2] a hog in my life until I come up here I have been compelled to kill them up here we always took them from union men when we could get them—Yes I forgot send me a loaf of light bread made of ~~short~~ shorts I want to have a big toast out of the sweet milk butter & light bread

I have not been in good health for several weeks I had the Flux[3] about 8 weeks ago & have had^the^ diarhea ever since or nearly so we have good clothing we have [3] good pair of pants 4 coats good boots though I believe our socks are about to run out. Send me a chew of tobacco & a pocket knife & all will be regular [?] tell ma and^all^of the family good evening for me I havent been drunk since I left now wont you send me the butter good bye for to night

John

NB Pa when you ~~direct~~ ^send^ your letters direct them Ft Smith capt Ross[4] com col Stones res Regiment McCulloch Brigade—Then we will get them by a direct express from there to our camps.

J.W.L.

1. The Minié Rifle was an important weapon in the mid-nineteenth century, especially on battlefields. It was named for French army captain Claude-Étienne Minié, who, along with Henri-Gustave Delvigne, developed the Minié ball to allow for rapid muzzle loading.

2. To steal or seize by stealth.

3. Dysentery.

4. Sam transfers regiments, switching from Wharton to Ross.

Letter 15

Camp Alcorn Hopkinsville Ky..
Decr 8th A. D. 1861
Jas M & T. A. Loves:

Dear parents:

This leaves myself in good health J.W Love is getting better of his complaint (Neuralgia[1]) Rob[t] High has Measles Uncle Andrew and young

Andy are as far as I can learn doing well— there are a great many of the Regiment sick of Measles Mumps or Pneumonia there are but few cases of Pneumonia but the Measles are of the worst kind five of the Freestone Co Company have died in about a week Mr Murray Strain David Clough and Stewart= before this reaches you Lincolns Message will possibly have reached you in which you will see that he calls for 700,000 more troops and $700,000,000 more of money and recommends the organization of the Northern Militia[2] = We have the report here that Price Reins and McCulloch[3] are concentrating their forces toward St. Louis and it is reported that the Federal forces have left Paduca and Cairo to go to the defence of S Louis they are Represented as being very much afraid that S[t] Louis will be taken

We have now and then a little excitement in camps— there was a report a day or two back that a strong Federal forc the first report was that 8000 of them were near Russelville the next report a short time after was 3000 but it finally proved to be some 200 of our own forces who had been in persuit of some 30 or 40 Kentucky Tories who had undertaken to burn the Rail Road bridge between Russelville and Clarksville the Road leads Northward toward Boling Green an Southward to Nashville the Roads from the other Southern States are so connected at the latter place as to afford great facilities for getting troops to Boling Green where it is thought they intend making an attack soon= I am of the opinion now that things will soon come to a head in this state and many who declare themselves to be unionists will have to get away from this region or take a different course from that which they are now persueing— they boast of their sentiments= A fellow by the name of Jackson left this place and went to the Northern Government became commander of a Regiment and says he intends to winter here— some of the women here say they will buy no goods until Jackson gets possession of the place A good many of the Unionists here are negro owners Lincolns Congress have possibly by this time passed an act by which they intend to set all negroes free and afterward to remunerate unionists for the losses they may sustain but the character of the expressions by which they signify their intention to pay the unionists what they may loose leads me to believe that they do not include the price of negroes in the payments this I suppose from the Lincoln Government considering the negro owner a unionist from interest only while his true sentiments are with the South It will be the best thing that can be for Kentucky for the Northern government to pass a law to free the negro every where in the South it will show to Ky that the other S. States have been right in considering this the great and only object of Abolitiondom although they have protested that keeping the union together= the Stars and Stripes was what they sought.[4]

We have preaching here twice every Sabbath and a pretty good sermon each time preaching is going on at this time in about fifty yards I understand from Kentuckyans that this has been a remarkably good winter up to this time= Our mess made up of Mr. G. T. Bradley as the head Capt Leroy and Marcellus Moody Wm Karris John Womack myself= and when they are here Col Gregg and Dr Alston are in tolerable health Burgess Modrell is doing very well I think something important will take place soon if so I will write to you= I have had but one letter from any of you that was from Terissa

Yours fraternally &c
C W Love

1. A pain in the nervous system caused by nerve damage.

2. At President Abraham Lincoln's request, on July 4, 1861, a special summer session of Congress appropriated $500 million to put five hundred thousand Union soldiers in the field.

3. Confederate Generals Sterling Price, Gabriel J. Rains, and Benjamin McCulloch.

4. On April 10, 1862, Congress declared that the federal government would compensate slave owners who freed their slaves.

Letter 16

Camp Alcorn— Hopkinsville Ky—
Dec^r.. 13th A.D. 1861
E.T.G. Love:

Dear Sister:

I received a letter from you some time back it was the only one I have had from any of you since I left home. I have written to father frequently this being sufficient as all would then know how we were getting along. I have learned nothing from the boys (Saml & John) more than what I wrote from Memphis. I have learned through Mr. Ja^s M. Davis of Springfield that Stones Regmt is possibly still at the same place they then were in the upper part of Arkansas. but I do not know enough about their location to know how to write to them. I do not know whether my letters reach you or not but I have expressed a desire in every letter to be informed where they are but as I get no letters from you I can know nothing about them. I have had a few chills within the last week and thought I had the Mumps but I do not know whether so or not if so they have been very light I am now getting well have not been under the necessity of going to bed for a good while during the time in fact hardly at all. Uncle Andrew Andrew jr and Robt High are at Clarksville Robt High has had Measles but is better I do not think there has been much the matter with Andrew jr at any time he has been like many others of the Company sick a little but generally low spirited There is a large Hospital at Clarksville a Female College with 150 rooms capable of accommodating from 400 to 600 men this Hospital the one here and all the hospital room at Nashville are full and crowded with the sick from this place and Boling Green there are about 5000 men here and about 50,000 at Boling Green. One of the Lynches has died= Bulger Peoples was very sick a few days ago= the man who told this k^n^ew Skruggs was there but could not tell about his health

This was a Mr Lenard from McClellan Co he is here to see one of his sons in this Regmt he has another son at Manassas himself and another son belong to Terry^s Regmt he says that from 75 to 100 of Terry^s men have died — A Mr Roberts who lives on Brazos Tiwacana is here— he has a son in the Company from McClellan County– There was a report here in Camp a couple of days ago that the army at Manassas had been falling back for four days burning their tents and breaking up their pot vessles and destroying all things else that they could not take with them this though is not to be believed any farther than that a strategetic move on the eve of a battle which is about to take place is being made by the Commanding Officers which may appear to men in some part of the line of Battle very much like a retreat= but I fully believe if there is any falling back at all it is for the purpose of having the advantage at some particular point= I am not able to get hold of more than half the News Papers that come to Camp and do not know whether the following report is from them or only verbal=Seward[1] is reported as having said that the people of his country would hear glorious news in a few days exactly what he meant by this is not known it may be that he thinks some great victory will be gained by the Federals but as they have been whipped every time and in view of this fact it could be considered nothing less than a high degree of presumption for him to allude to such a thing as this the glorious news must in my view be the hanging of Slidell and Mason[2] as they have these men in a defenseless condition in their power and I understand hold such a threat over them in fact they are trying to have acts passed by their Congress to confine them in dungeons from some statements in the last papers we have it appears that Price and McCulloch[3] having of Offices of equal grade and one not willing to obey the other there has been an officer placed in command over both the same paper states that Price is moving toward Kansas where the same report says he intends making his future operations but I do not believe this at all There have up to this time Eight if not Ten of our company dead the last one is now being buried at this place the two that possibly make up the ten are at Clarksville. Uncle Andrew stated in a letter to Col Gregg that he had a temporary position in the Hospital at Clarksville— Mr. Davis came by there as he came here he says Uncle Andrew is pretty much worn out by his assiduity in attending to the sick

I have not written to anyone else but father before this and will write to him hereafter as money is too scarce to be spending much no more should be spent than is necessary to make our health and circumstances known at home

I have written about all worthy writing about and possibly a good deal more and will quit hoping to get a letter from home soon[4]

Yours truly &c.
C.W. Love

1. William H. Seward (1801-1872) served as US Secretary of State from 1861 to 1869.

2. James Mason and John Slidell were confederate diplomats in Britain involved in the "Trent Affair" also known as the "Mason and Slidell Affair" in which the union ship San Jacinto intercepted the RMS Trent confiscating both men as contrabands of war as well as correspondence between Britain and the Confederacy.

3. It was well known that McCulloch and Price did not get along, as Cyrus alludes to in this letter.

4. The bottom portion of the letter was apparently torn before the writing of the letter and does not obstruct any of the words on the page.

Letter 17

Camp Alcorn Hopkinsville Ky—
Decr the 18th A.D. 1861

Dear Father & Mother:

I am now writing on a soapbox across my lap by candlelight. Since I last wrote I have been improving in health and may say that I am entirely well with the exception of bad cold which appears to act on me as on all the balance of the Regmt: it seems to take hold of the Lungs more than I have ever noticed before I weighed myself this evening and weighed 140 lb having fallen off in flesh in the course of 3 or 4 weeks to this weight from 145 lb. There is at this time not so much sickness in the Regmt as has been but what has been has produced serious in roads on the numbers of the Regmt upwards of 40 have died since we left Texas and ten of that number have been from our company= those that have died are the following: M.J.Clough. Alex Strain. Peyton Murray. John W David. Young Petty.

8 at this place and Liuet Oliver Burleson and Mr Oliver at Clarks=ville and I consider 3 or 4 more in a dangerous condition I shall not call the names of any particular persons except in a case like this in which I will say that I do not wish you to mention names so they will be heard of from their relatives at least until I write again= I heard from Clarks=ville a day or two ago: young Mr Anderson formally an editor of the Pioneer was at Clarksville and brought information that uncle A.C.: A.C. jr and Robt High were in good health or improving Uncle Andrew wrote here about a week ago that he was in a very good temporary position in the Hospital at Clarksville and I understand from those who have come from there at various times since the establishment of the Hospital that he has pretty nearly exhausted his powers of endurance by his constant attention to the sick=Robt Murray is still at Clarksville= he has applied for a discharge and I think will get it as the Physicians there have certified to his

being disqualified for service by the effect of Measles on his lungs= several cases of Measles have caused death in the same way by affecting the lungs I have still had but one letter from any of you the news here is dull generally=there is however some fighting going on around here= there was a fight a day or two ago up in Western Virginia in which our forces 1200 strong are said to have whipped 5000 of the enemy= there is a report here that a skirmishing fight took place near Boling Green in which we are said to have whipped them capturing 300 of their cavalry the first fight is published being official the latter was telegraphed to this place last night= There is a report also that Jim Jackson[1] intends taking his Christmas dinner at this place he may attempt to do so but if he succeeds it will be after he finds himself in charge of Confederate troops he dos not know possibly that there are enough Confederate forces here to whip anything he can bring against us= it appears that from 6000 to 10000 were in about 50 miles of us a night or two ago but I do not know whether to believe it or not= don't care if its so

I write here by the light of a green Red Oak fire the fire part having been very necessary and comfortable for these many nights passed. We are now in a new camp On the Nashville Road about a mile and half nearly South from Town= we were formally about a half mile West of Town they have very nice streams of water in this section of country the whole understrata here seems to be lime and marble and Sink Holes and caves are numerous foxes seem to be plenty as I would judge from hearing dogs run them now and then at Princeton there is a fine branch running through the earth and only two places at which it is accessible as far as learned one of them in the edge of the town the other some 300 or 400 yds from that where it empties into a large creek

I stated in my other letter that cousin John[2] was getting on very well but of late he does not seem to improve but rather to decline he has been afflicted with Neuralgia of the face and in the last day or two his bowels have been running off he is now talking of going to Clarksville and I think he would do well to go for a while The clothing for our company has not yet got to hand but we are looking for it every day Mr Davis went from here to Boling Green. A Mr Lenard who was in camps a few days ago says that from 75 to 100 of Terrys Regmt had died—there are as far as I can learn at least 50000 men in and about Boling

We have plenty of good beef. Flour bread and genuine coffee the latter not mixt with either rie or corn meal Barley or Chocolate= Beef at 12 ½ cts per lb now and then once a week we have bacon=Once or twice since we have been here a little pork and sassengers= this is a land of porkers (Bacon from 25 ^cts^ to 30 ^cts^ pr ^lb^ pork 10 ^cts^ gross)[3]

Two or three of the men of our Regmt have been found asleep on their posts= Genl Clark had the different Regmts of Infantry 5 in Number in general review day before yesterday at the end of review he said on account of the men not having been informed fully as to their duties he would spare them but that after that time the man who went to sleep on post should certainly be shot (I hope he has scared those fully who are inclined to sleep) he said also that he expected us to have a fight in a few days with forces of the enemy fully equal in numbers to ours if we should I feel fully confident we will by the favor of the Almighty (whose favor is not with the many or the few but with the just cause) give them more than they bargained for

I am inclined to think Lincolns Message and the appearance of things in the present Federal Congress will turn many a union man in both Kentucky and Tennessee in fact the last papers state that in one of the strongest Union counties in East Tenn the unionists are now raising an Regmt for the Confederate service Nothing more now= except that Burgess Modrell is doing very well personally but has no more pleasure in outside affairs than I have

Hoping the Almighty will bless all your family at home and elsewhere I remain yours in filial regard

C.W. Love

1. Union brigadier general James S. Jackson, presumably the same Jackson mentioned in Letter 15.

2. Cousin John W. Love (not to be confused with cousin John Webb or John Wilson Love, Cyrus's younger brother) enlisted along with Cyrus in the Seventh Regiment Texas Infantry under Colonel Moody in Fairfield.

3. The equivalent of the prices in 2015 dollars would be beef $3.20 per pound, bacon $6.40-$7.70 per pound, and pork $2.50 per pound.

Letter 18

Camp Alcorn Hopkinsville Ky
Jany 8th A.D. 1862

Dear Tea:— I recd your letter of Decr 18th this morning it was in one of those long brown envelopes from it for the first time since we left home I learned something of the boys — I learned that they were yet in the land of the living if one in a soldiers life can be said to be living I can hardly feel that he is though, for he is rather draging out a miserable existence I wish you would write to me at all times on receiving any information of them Until I received your letter I had not been able to know whether Stones Regmt was in the fight at Belmont or not and have therefore been very uneasy. This leaves me Uncle A.C. who is attending the sick at the Hospitals in this place and A.C. jr in tolerable good health. Geo Blain is also in good health.— Cousin John W. is not entirely healthy his being affected by neuralgia — I do not know whether I said so in my last letter to father or not– but John is trying to get a discharge from the service at the present time with the design of going to a private house somewhere near this place and taking a course of medicine under the charge of Dr Alston otherwise he is not in bad health[1] — Robt High is at Clarksville is not in good health having had Measles. he is also home sick and I think he is more affected by the latter complaint than the former — he is however in a condition that he will not able to do any service this Winter — his Uncle (Mosely) from Alabama came up to see if he could not procure a discharge for him but did not succeed in doing that

I think he then tried to get a furlow for him but Genl Clark will not grant furlows in but very few instances when they are known to be unfit to do service he has given discharges in about twenty instances for men of this Regmt. there were Seven Hundred and thirty nine of our Regmt when it was organized at this place — there are now or rather were reported by this mornings muster roll to be Six Hundred and nine of all the men thus missing from the Regmt there are only about the twenty that were discharged living making about One Hundred and nineteen that have died which is about One Sixth of the Regmt.

We are camped here on low ground near the bank of a bold running creek which is very good water at all other times than when we have had rains sufficient to run on the roads and wash mud into it we then have as muddy water as you ever see in a creek we are now living in huts made of Red Oak slabs and our tents for a roof. they are comfortable and warm but when it rains this whole country is very disagreeably muddy. Some of the messes in the different companies of the Regmt have made their bunks which answer in the place of bedsteads– My mess have not got theirs made yet and if it continues rainy and bad weather as it has been to day and for some time past we will not be able to make them for just that length of time as we cannot until the weather is fair move our bedding out of the house and with it and the clothing in the house tere being so much of it we can do nothing. All the clothing and bedding sent to us has got here except possibly one box which has by some means been misplaced and we do not know where it is likely to be — Cousin J. W. L brought two of them and says there were six at Clarksville we got three of the four yesturday and understand that the other was put on the same wagon it may have been treated like some of the things in one of the boxes and in J. H. Colletts trunk some of the things sent to young Burleson were possibly stolen and Colletts trunk was broken open and an overcoat of his and one belonging to Wm [McIlvien] were stolen — I got an overcoat a vest one pr socks one shirt one neck comfort and one bed comfort and a pr shoes — I have now more clothing than know what to do with a coat like the one I got would cost at this place twelve or fifteen dollars the vest eight or ten the shoes about five and every thing in the way of clothing costs in proportion about like these common letter paper like this I write on costs fifty cts at Clarksville no kind can be had at this place.[2] Since we have got to this place we are not visited very often by the young ladies from town. they were at our camp the other side of town nearly every day as it was but half a mile off — We have been very badly treated by the chief physician of this brigade he has neglected the sick in a most wanton manner rarely ever seeing any of them himself and has not had the Hospitals kept clean atall they smell exceedingly bad and in the old hospital there have to his and everyone elses knowledge been a great number of body lice which he has taken no pains to have destroyed. they have had hardly any medicine here until today this however may have been to our advantage. this chief physicians name is Lile[3] and and from his language and actions it seems to have been his chief object to show his power and authority at the Hospitals by rudely treating all the sick men he might happen to see and by insulting with sirly language threats of arrest and the publication of notices at the doors of the Hospitals — That no commissioned ^officer^ should go in except at certain hours of the day and not then unless ^they^ had first got the presence of a physician who belonged to the Medical Staff to conduct them about the rooms– Some of these commissioned officers however have concluded not to bear with him any longer — Some of them have cursed the whole concern General, Medical Staff and all, others have intimated things of a serious character to Dr Lisle and one that I know of sais if if Lisle will just speak cross to him he kill him in an instant he was insulted by him two or three times and once in circumstances which he will not easily forgive many of them say they would rather kill him than an enemy from the Lincoln Government.

Mrs. Gregg has been at the house of one of her kinsmen by the name of Garth for about two months but has possibly by this time gone home to her fathers in Alabama; she has been sick the most of the time since She came here caused no doubt by over exertion in attending the sick at Clarksville when she first came. You did not inform me when you wrote whether the boys were in anything like comfortable circumstances or not I wish when you answer this you would say something about it if you know I am sorry to learn of the death of Harriet but it is possibly best for her.

I hope Grandfather[4] will live till I get back if Providence permits me to get throug this war — home and its comforts with all the hard labor that may be necessary to procure those comforts are rich blessing hardly ever properly appreciated by those who have them — it seems to me nothing would give me more pleasure than to be at home with father attending to all domestic affairs as they came to hand But if I am permitted by a kind Providence on whom we should at all times rely to live three years longer these three years may have to be spent in a soldiers life in the camp[5] Tea if you wish to have a relish for the best of Books read your bible every day it has more important and truthful history both sacred and profane concerning the character and genealogy of mankind than a hundred thousand times the same amount of print in any other book in the knowledge of our race Writing of such thing as the most of that on the preceding pages I could finish out a good many pages but I will write no more of them — I have but little local news and you get General news faster than I can get it here — With the hope that you will all write to me often I will ceas this letter.

Yours fraternally &c.
C.W. Love

P.S. Have you none but long envelopes in your country[6]

1. According to the muster cards, Cousin John W. Love was discharged on January 7, 1862, in Hopkinsville.

2. Although Confederate inflation should be taken into consideration, in 2015 this is the equivalent of $12.75.

3. Most likely Dr. George Lisle from Labette County in Kansas.

4. Most likely the paternal grandfather, Joseph Love.

5. Confederate Provisional Congress reenlistment law explained that a volunteer signing up for a three-year term would receive a furlough of sixty days, a bounty of fifty dollars, and the ability to determine his own arm of the service. Volunteers could leave a unit if they so desired and could elect their own officers.

6. About two-thirds of the page is left blank on this letter. There are mathematical calculations under the postscript.

Letter 19

Camp Alcorn Hopkinsville Ky = Jany 15th 1862
Miss E.T.G.Love

Dear Sister:—I received your letter of Decr 22nd a day or two ago from which I gather the information that you had recd other letters from the boys since you wrote it appears that they are with Price at Springfield Mo.. whether McCulloch is at that place^ or not you did not say^ there has not to my knowledge been any fighting in Mo yet we can hardly get the truth about anything here — I answered your other letter the same day it got to hand — I mean the one in the long envelope which was unsealed when it came to hand and did not have the appearance of having been sealed atall you should be careful to seal your letters if you do not wish them to be read ^by^ others than those you write to In your last — the one this is an answer to you say that Joe Baker wrote to his father that he had not had his coat on during the day that he wrote and that it was the first cold weather he had experienced since he had got into that country of any consequence. The coldest weather we have had here was yesturday the day before and today so far — there has been a little snow and sleet but not enough to cover the ground and there has been but little wind with it except the first day when there was a little bluster from the North attended with some rain but it did not last long I believe however that it has been greatly to our disadvantage that we have had so warm and mild a winter tho little changes from cold to warm with the attendant dampness of the atmosphere has no doubt in my mind been the cause of so much sickness and death among us —The Reg^{mt} has lost up to this time about One Hundred and thirty men by death and about twenty five by discharge several have gone home from the Reg^{mt} on furlough to try to get recruits for the Reg^{mt} — I cannot however believe that there will be many recruits except from purely patriotick motives if the true state of things here is fairly represented to them they will at once see that their chances for dying of camp diseases is far greater than the chances of being killed on the field of battle– Sickness in the camp seems to be somewhat abated though not much=and from what those who have been living in this country a long time say this has been a milder winter than usual up to this time but the worst of it is from about the first of this month on up to March if this should be the case this winter we have nearly all the cold part of it to go through yet=but it may not be the intention to bring recruits here until Spring opens which I think is the proper time for Soldiers from the more Southern States to come I shall write a letter to Saml & john soon maybe it will get to them — write to me at all times immediately on receiving any news from them — a letter has just been recd from Jas Davis who was at Boling Green when he wrote he went from here to Boling Green to take clothes to the Limestone Co Boys. when he got there he waited a while to see the big fight which was supposed would take place right away but had not up to the time of his writing he took sick after he went up there and after waiting some time for the fight concluded to start back home which he did some days ago I expect if so he may reach home before this letter gets to you in his letter from Boling Green he says the Limestone County boys had not died as badly as we had heard =we had had heard that one of the Lynch boys and one of the Peoples boys also were dead: but he stated that Peoples was not dead had been sick but was [then] so he could go about — I am now in the house of a Mr Bryan waiting on Geo Bradley Jno Womack and Georges old negro Cy. George has been threatened with inflammation of the Brain and since he got better of that he has been having periodical chills and fevers—he is not yet clear of his brain affection—the chills are abut seven and fourteen days apart today was his day to have one but so far it seems to me he has had no signs of it and I think he will miss it entirely Jno Womack has been affected by a combination of diseases he is however nearly clear of most of them but will never be fit for service and I doubt if he will ever become able to walk much– he says his back was broke when he was a boy and that he has never been well of it since at this time he is unable to turn himself over in bed and we have to be careful in moving him to keep from hurting him.

Geo Blain is acting commissary[1] for the Reg^{mt} and is generally busy coming and going to and from the camp to town for provisions — Uncle A.C. is in the Hospital hard at work waiting on the sick of the Reg^{mt} as far as he is able. A.C. jr & Cousin John are Staying at camp for the time in my mess Andrew has been sick as I stated in a previous letter but was better until six or eight days ago when he took the Mumps he is getting better of them now Robt High is still at Clarksville=a few days before we got to Monroe La John Balch a son of Parson Balch who once preached for East Prairie folks got with us since he got here he has larned that his father who it seems had been inclined to consumption for some time has died John is now trying to get a discharge for the purpose of going home to take care of his mother but I do not know whether he will be able to procure one or not. Co^{l} Gregg has written on to the war department to get one for him if it can be done but has not received any information yet as to what would be done in the case– Mssrs Leroy & Marcellus Moody are getting well Capt Moody has been suffering from Flux for the last five or six days but I think was some better this morning Mr W.T. Harris Has had Measles which have affected his head or rather his ears one of them has been running for several days= Burgess Modrell has been in pretty good health ever since he has been here — I would like very much to see you all for a few days and then come back again=tell Ellen[2] if I stay the three years out I will expect to see more besides herself and Jim[3] about= what I have to eat I told you in a previous letter give me all the news of the country when you answer this — Yours fraternally ~~C.W. Love~~

C.W.Love.

C W Love [T. T.] A Love [4]

1. A person commissioned to gather supplies from local residents.

2. Ellen Love is married to James A. Love, making her Cyrus's sister-in-law.

3. James A. Love, his brother.

4. This letter has some additional writing in a lighter ink or pencil on the top and bottom margins of the second page. On the top, "C.W. Love" is written three times along with "Tennie" and "Tennie Love." At the bottom, "C W Love" and "[T T.] A Love" are written upside down. The handwriting appears to be Cyrus's, though these marginal notes may have been added by Tea, the letter's recipient.

Letter 20

Camp Washington Jany the[1] 1862

Dear Sister[2]

Yours of the 29th of Dec came to hand to day & I proceed to answer it immediately.

I was ~~v~~ very sorry to hear of the sickness of Capt. Moody[s] company and very sorry to hear of the death of so many of the boys .. but it is the fate of war & the adge is true that disease takes off more than the sword .. for there has .. more than 40 of this Regt died of disease .. while there has'nt been but 5 killed and 12 or 15 wounded in our late battle on the head waters of the Vertigres River .. called the battle of Chewstinella[3] .. however I hope .. the next time I hear from you to hear of Cy and Andrew[s] entire recovery from the measles & mumps .. also I want you to write me .. how to direct a letter to Cy. I received a letter from Tea stating that Grandfather & aunt ~~m~~ Mary were very sick & I feared .. the next letter I received would bring news of the death of one or both of them but I was very glad to hear by your letter that they were both recovering .. Tea also wrote me word that Hariet was dead.. I was very sorry to hear it for she was a faithful negro. There is but little sickness in this Regt. at this time though there has been a great many cases of the measles and mumps and some few cases of the pneumonia but no case of the Small pox yet .. and I hope it will not get into this Regt. atall not= withstanding it is at Fort Smith Some 25 miles distant from this place. I have writen to Tea twice Since we returned from the campaign and battle and in one of them {{the first}} I give as full a discription of the battle as I could & you must make her send you that letter if you wish to read a <u>full discription</u> of the battle however I will give you a short description of the ~~battle~~ it. After cooking 4 days provision on the night of the 25 Dec {{I made biscuit for near 3 hours without stopping}} we set out on the morning of the 26th {{while one of the coldest northers I ever felt come full in our faces}} to see if we could find the enemy {{I forgot to say that we were drawn up in line of battle on the evening of the 25th on account of the Indian pickets to the amount of 200 or 300 running ours of 40 into camps .. and our pickets reported the enemy to the amount of 5000 or 6000 drawn up in line of battle behind a long ridge Some three miles off .. Co[l] Greer's Reg[t]. under command of Lt Co[l] Lane was sent forward as the advance to bring on the fight with Co[l] Stone[s] Reg[t] to support him under command of Lt. Col Griffith while Co[l's] Young & M[c]Entoshes Reg[t's] Supported the first two .. but the report was false or else they moved off behind the ridge so we could not see them All the time we were drawn up we could see their Spies come to the top of the ridge and then return and then some more would come up .. It was thought to be Spies of the party that run our pickets in}} .. and after traveling about 12 miles we crossed a large creek and directly after we saw a large smoke .. Some said Indians while others laughed at the idea myself among the latter and soon after we saw the Smoke I took a biscuit & piece of pork out of my pocket an and after dividing it with my file partner We commenced ~~ea~~ eating and laughing at the idea of getting into a battle for just as we commenced eating the order was given to cap our guns .. but our Skepticism did not last long for we had'nt gone more than 200 yds before we heard a gun fire toward the van of the army and then 3 or 4 and then 15 or 20 and directly about 300 or 400 along a line of something near 3/4 of a mile .. after that my friend said Sam that sounds like battle .. they were firing at the advance guard under Capt Short of Col Greer's Regt though none of their balls took effect for they were Shooting 400 or 500 yds. The order of the battle was as follows ..the Indians occupied the top of a very steep and almost inaccesible hill with very large rocks all over the side of it .. There was 300 Seminoles and 200 Osages and Creeks making 500 on the top of that hill and they had pledged themselves to hold it or die, and they could have held it if they could have stood a charge like white men for our little army of 1[2]80 could have held it against 10,000 drilled troops .. this 500 were sustained by about 2000 in the valley back of them .. and now to the order of battle on our side. Co^{l} Griffith was ordered to the right= to dismount and charge the hill on foot while Co$^{l's}$ Lane and McEntosh$^{'es}$ Reg$^{t's}$ were ordered to the center and Co^{l} Young to the left {{ Co^{l} McEntosh commanding}}. After all was formed the order to charge was sounded by the bugle .. Co$^{l's}$ Lane Young and McEntosh$^{'es}$ Reg^{ts} charged gallantly on horse back while we charged through a creek about 1 1/2 ft in water and ice ~~an~~ and the same in mud= but when we got to the top of the bank on the opposite side from where we started our Co^{l} saw that we would not get into the fight on foot so he took the responsibility of ordering us back to our horses .. So we charged through the creek again and got back to our horses but we were so exhausted that we could hardly mount our horses but when we did we made them git faster for the other Regts had got the Start of us and were likely to gain the laurels of the day.. but by moving to the right and charging another hill we got the lead and killed about as many as Co^{l} Greer's & Youngs and more than the Arkansawyers did however we did not get off without getting 4 killed and 12 to 14 wounded in this Regt among those killed was Lt Fitsu of Capt Throgmortons co who is very much regretted by the whole Reg^{t} and Thos= Arnold of Waco Capt Rosses Co they were both shot in the brain and both died bravely .. young Arnold killed the Indian that killed Lt Fitsu and just as he was killed he killed an Indian that wounded a Mr Whittington of Capt R^{s} co Mr W= at the same time killing the Idian that killed young Arnold. I will close this part of my letter.. for.. as I told you I ~~did not~~ ^do not^ intend to give a full account of the battle in this. but Tea will get one with a full account of it. The Indians loss is from 300 to 400 Betty I have not received but three letters since I left home one from Mr Vanhorn one from Tea and one from you. I have not written very many letters myself but I could not.. for we have been on the march at least 5/6 of the time since we left Texas and have traveled not less than 5000 or 6000 miles. I have once been ~~w~~ within 100 miles of St Louis. But notwithstanding all that I have written some 12 or 15 letters to the family .. all to Tea and father. If I dont write to all of you while I am on the march it is no fault of mine for it is all I ~~cad~~ can do to write atall.. but while I am in winter quarters I will try to write to all I can. I know I ought to have written to you but I thought you would learn all from Tea^{s} and fathers letters.. as well as how to direct your letters. So you see that it was not because I did not wish to write to you .. but because I could not help it very well .. And now I intend to propose a plan by which you may all hear from me when I am on the march as well as for me to hear from you. It is this I will write firs to one and then to the other and when the one written to receives it you will Seal it and Send it ~~to~~ to the other .. both writing as soon as you receive it. Now this seems a little selfish but it is not for {{ as I said before it is impossible for me to write many letters when I am on the march 1st because I cannot carry the material and 2nd because I have not got the time .. but notwithstanding all this I will write as often as I can and while I am in winter quarters I will write to all I can.. For my greatest pleasure is in receiving and reding letters .. and all my friends sem to think that I should open a correspondence instead of Studying the disadvantages under which I labor .. They.. may also think that they ought not to write because I cannot write to all of them in a different letter but where I have a number of ~~friend~~ friend in one town or neighborhood I could write to them all in one and by that means keep up a correspondence with several towns and neighborhoods and ~~al~~ also keep them informed about what is going on here. Tell them to write .. as many of them as will and if they will not be satisfied without me writing to all of them I will try to write to all that write to me. I will now close this part of my letter and give a few items about the army the War and Gen Mcullough. In the first place something near 10,000 troops ^are^ quartered in this state composing Gen Mculloughs brigade ^it is^ composed of 4 Reg^{ts} Texas cavalry 3 Reg^{ts} mounted riflemen of Ark^ansian^{s}^ = 3 or 4 Reg^{ts} Infantry and two battalions .. one from Tex and the other from Ark .. 4 Reg^{ts} are camped on the Ark River and the others on White River. It is thought.. here by all the wise ones that we will make a move towards St Louis or [?] Kansas. I cannot conjecture what we will do but one thing is certain if we can ever come up with those rascally dutch we will give them such a thrashing that I think they will be sorry they ever commenced this unnatural war. It is said that Seigel[4] has resigned but it is not credited here. The United States have succeeded one commander with another in rapid succession ever since we have been in the Service 1st Fremont then Hunter and then Holleck who now commands. Betty I have continued this letter farther now than I intended to with a great deal that will not be of any interest to you so I will close it as soon as possible. By stating in reference to Gen Mcullough that he is one of the worst slandered men I ever saw and the truth is he has been lied on generally.[5] The government has endorsed all his proceedings here.

One thing I forgot to mention .. that while we were forming the Indians were barking like a dog howling like a wolf & yelling and gobbling like a Turkey. This leaves us all well and doing very well and I do hope this long but badly written letter will find you all enjoying the same blessing. give Give my Love to all enquiring friends and accept the love of your brother .. Sam ..Lou[6] your Small note was very thankfully received and would have been more so if it had been longer. but I think you will do better next time .. and be shure you do'nt let the shortness of my note be an excuse for not writing me a long one for I have nothing to write you more than I have written to your Aunt Betty .. except for you to give my love to all the girls of Fairfield for God bless them I Love them all .. it is them that make a home worth having and life a blessing.

Lou you must not criticise this letter to closely for it is badly written and worse it is badly put together.

So now I must close but before I do accept the kindest regards of your friend

Sam.. Love

1. Based on the date Sam received the incoming letter from Mary Elizabeth Karner and assuming at least two weeks for delivery to Limestone County, this letter was likely written around the fifteenth of January 1862.

2. The letter was sent to Mary Elizabeth Karner (Sam calls her Betty).

3. The Battle of Chustenahlah, fought near the Verdigris River in Oklahoma. The battle, a Confederate victory, pitted Southern troops against pro-Union Native Americans and was fought in what was Indian territory at the time.

4. German Union officer Franz Sigel was best known for the Battle of Pea Ridge in March of 1862, a Union victory.

5. General McColloch was an eccentric personality who was known to dislike General Price and was also known to have a strong distaste for army uniforms. His eccentricities may be the cause for the "slander" Sam refers to

here.

6. Possibly Louetta Karner, Mary Elizabeth and John's daughter.

Letter 21

After a long hiatus spent in winter quarters, the Union army began to advance in mid-January, earning minor victories in Kentucky at Middle Creek on January 10 and Mills Spring on January 19. This positioned the Federals, under Ulysses S. Grant, to move up the Tennessee River, as mentioned in paragraph three of Cyrus's letter below. The accounts Cyrus provides of the Battle of Middle Creek in this letter are not historically accurate.

Hopkinsville Ky.
Jany 22nd 1862
John & Elizabeth Karners

Dear brother & sister: This leaves me and the other relatives here in good health except colds. I have cold the second time for the last five or six days which like the first seems to ^have^ deep hold on my lungs= there have about one hundred and forty of the Regmt died since we came here — Leoroy & Marcellus Moody Geo Bradley and John Womack are considerably better John Womack will however be confined to his bed for a good while yet on account of the weakness of his loins

Capts Moody and W.T. Harris are in camps the Capt has had a slight attack of flux but is better Harris had Measles which settled in his head and finally broke in his ear as the ear got better the Mustles of his neck swelled an is paining him very much I think from its appearance it will break in a few days

There have been a good many reports of the advance of the enemy since we came here a report came six or eight days ago that they were certainly advancing on us and were reported by Couriers to be in about thirty five miles of us and the calculation was that we would have had a fight here three or four days ago but Col Forest[1] who went out with about a thousand men has returned and reports the enemy at South Carrolton but he did not know if it were their design to come this way as they seem to be undetermined themselves I believe they are afraid to come although from all appearances this seems to be the time at which they have concluded to make their long contemplated simultaneous movements

We had the report about the same time that the enemys gun boats had come up the Tennessee river and taken Fort Henry and were also marching on Fort Donaldson[2] on the Cumberland river. We have also a report that they had attacked Humphrey Marshal in the Mountains of East Kentucky the first report was that Marshal had whipped them in the fight but from an insufficiency of forces was under the necessity of falling back farther into the Mountains — the last report is taken from a yankee paper stating that Marshal considering his case a desperate one had given his men choice between a fight and disbanding they are said to have chosen the latter disbanded and were trying to make their excape as best they could the Yankee paper stated that they were being persued by a strong force of cavalry There is no doubt of the Confederates forces in N.W. Virginia having driven the enemy in complete route to the North Side of the Potomac they also took U.S. Munitions and provisions to the amount in value of about three hundred thousand dollars — from the best information I can get there are above One Hundred thousand men at Boling Green — they will be certain to whip any force that can come against them. There are several of our company who have made application for discharges or are about to do so Robt Murrays discharge has just come to hand John Bolchs has been applied for and has been looked for for several days John Womack will necessarily get one

Our Company at this time numbers rank & file [at] seventy one men we have lost twenty three by death and two by discharge– there is but little severe sickness but a good deal of light sickness for the last week or two nothing more

Yours &c.
C.W.Love

1. Colonel Nathan Bedford Forrest was known for innovation in his cavalry tactics and was called a "wizard" in the saddle. He became the first grand wizard of the Ku Klux Klan and was accused of war crimes against the black soldiers fighting for the United States during the Battle of Fort Pillow. For more information regarding Nathan Bedford Forrest or the Founding of the Ku Klux Klan, see *White Terror: The Ku Klux Klan Conspiracy and Southern Reconstruction* by Allen W. Trelease.

2. The actual name of the fort is Donelson.

Letter 22

We surmise that this letter fragment was written between January 16, 1862, and January 29, 1862, based on the position of Union forces near Fort Henry. The Battle of Fort Henry did not occur until February 2, 1862, which means that the letter must have been written prior to this date.

In this fragment and the next letter, Cyrus mentions the name Crittenden several times. Two Crittenden brothers, sons of Senator John J. Crittenden of Kentucky, fought on opposite sides in the war. George B. Crittenden was a brigadier general in the Confederate army, as was Felix Zollicoffer, whom Cyrus also mentions. George's brother, Thomas Leonidas Crittenden, and his cousin, Thomas Turpin Crittenden, were both generals in the Union army. Thomas Leonidas was in command of the Fifth Division of the Army of Ohio, which fought its first battle at Mills Spring. Thomas Turpin was nearby as well, as he spent the winter of 1861-1862 near Bowling Green.

There are none of the Reg^{mt} dying at this time I think and none have died in the last eight or ten days the Reg^{mt} has suffered severe loss of numbers but we have not suffered as much as a Kentucky Battalion at this place they have lost as I learn One Hundred & the rise since they came here out of about five hundred. Some of the Mississippi Reg^{mts} have lost more in proportion to numbers than we have and the people who live here have been dying of the same diseases.

Our Adjutant has been to Boling Green Nashville & Clarksville. he says there is no prospect of a fight at Boling G. that he learned of. While at Nashville a telegraphic dispatch came from N. O. to the effect [that] England had recognized the Southern Confederacy and that it was generally believed at that place. The movement of Crittendens forces was not to come immediately to this place as was thought for a while: they went to a place (South Carrolton) on [Green][1] River and were there the last that was known of them what their design is can hardly be conjectured but we will be able to meet and whip them let them come which [way they][2] may I think.

There are about 25,000 of the enemys forces in near Fort Henry on the Tennessee River. Who I think have put themselves in a rather close place if they could only know it We have a report here that Price in Missouri has whipped and captured a force of S 10,000 of the enemy and it is believed but may not be true: There is also report that a battle has been fought and won by the Confederates on the Potomac but this is not believed There are but Six of our company now at Clarksville and but two in the Hospital at this place. Robt. Williams is in bad health and has been for some time—he has decreased in flesh very much—has been sick a long time—nearly ever since we came here. he does not take as good care of himself as he Should and unless some change takes place I doubt if he will ever get well Most of the boys of our company are in camp and but few who are not getting better but there are not more than eight or ten able to do military duty and none of them much more than able There are considerable fortifications being made at Clarksville and Nashville The people of the latter place are said to be very much afraid the enemy will get as far down as that place but there fears are I think entirely groundless. After Crittendens and Zollicoffers defeat. Crittenden conducted the retreat of his forces across Cumberland River and has made a stand in about nineteen miles of the place where the fight took place with the determination to fight them again he having received reinforcements will no doubt whip them if they engage in battle. There will no doubt be some hard fighting as soon as the weather is suitable for infantry and Artillery to move. the weather at this time is very bad and changes oftener than it does in Texas it has been raining all day and has sleeted some to night it is sleeting and raining together at this time about ten Oclock

I wrote in my last letter to you that Forest[s] cavalry forces had been out. There is a man with Forest[s] forces who fights on his own hook. When Forrest returned he left this man to watch the movements of the enemy. He took it into his head to try to kill some of the enemys pickets at a bridge near where they are now staying—hiched his horse about three miles from the bridge and went to it found three of them there killed two of them broke one of their guns—took the other and came in a day or two ago—some other independent men are doing similar acts

What I have written is not of much importance as you will no doubt have heard the most of it before this reaches you. Burgess is well and doing well he sends his respects to all.

Yours fraternally
C.W. Love

1. An ink spot obscures this word.
2. An ink spot obscures these words.

Letter 23

In this letter, Cyrus describes the Battle of Mills Spring, Kentucky. As he states, Confederate Generals Felix Zollicoffer and George Crittenden were defeated. Zollicoffer mistook enemy soldiers for his own and rode up to them ordering them to stop firing on fellow Confederates. Historical accounts corroborate Cyrus's story, though he gets some of the details wrong. See Days of Glory *by Larry J. Daniel.*

It is possible that Cyrus has mixed up the towns of Calhoun and Carrolton in Kentucky in this letter and Letter 22. Calhoun is located near the Green River and is roughly sixty miles from Hopkinsville, where Cyrus is stationed.

Camp Alcorn Hopkinsville Ky
Jany 27th A.D. 1862
Jas M & TA Loves:

Dear father and Mother:

I have not written to you in some time but have written to Tirissa & others so you have heard from me.

This leaves myself and the other relatives and acquaintance in good health and with plenty of clothing and bedding to be comfortable and plenty to eat of beef Flour bread genuine coffe & sugar and whatever else we may be able to purchase when we have the money which just at this time is very scarce generally and with me the last of the $48.00 with which I left home was spent this morning for the unnecessary comfort called tobacco. I think it will however be but a few days until we will be paid about One Months wages[1] which will possibly be about sufficient to feed a man a few times on butter eggs chickens and some other little things bought with this money at from thirty to thirty five pr ct discount and with Tenn money at a Discount of 40 to 50 pr ct Discount this is because the whole trade of the country of almost all kinds is in the hands of Unionists with whom this whole country is [owned]. I am fully of the opinion that if the war is brought into this region of country it will truly be a war of brother against brother and of son against father [as] in many instances the children of the same family are in both armies. there are several cases in this region one family in particular the father being a rabid Unionist has two sons in the Northern Army & one in the Southern at Boling Green—there are numberless instances of this kind in this Christian County. It appears now that the Northern forces have begun the long threatened Simultaneous movement against us. About 27,000 of them from report have taken Murray in Tennessee and it appears are getting in the rear of Fort Henry. there is hardly any doubt now of their having whipped Crittenden & Zollicoffer up in the Mountains of East Ky and that they the last that was heard of them were retreating toward Knoxville Tenn—and that the enemy were possibly in Tenn in persuit of them. The report of the battle the way we have it is that the enemy had crossed a creek called fish Creek to the No of fifteen hundred (this was reported to Crittenden) he supposed or rather heard that they could not cross any more because of the creek having risen considerably with this impression Crittenden ordered Zollicoffer to attack them he did so but instead of 1500 he found fifteen or twenty thousand during the fight Zollicoffer rode up to a regiment which he supposed was one of his that were firing on another one of his and ordered them to cease firing as they were killing their own men—the regiment he rode up to was an Indiana Reg^{mt}.

Zollicoffer did not discover his Mistake until the Co^{l} of the Reg^{mt} rode up to him Z. immediately drew his sword and killed the Col but he and all his Staff were immediately fired on by the reg^{mt} Zollicoffer and several of his Staff were killed the others were wounded Z.^{s} forces then

The Ramsey family, summer 1903. A hatless Tennessee Love stands front and center. Left to right: *Annie Ramsey, Ruby Ramsey, cousin Johnny Karner, Louise Ramsey, C.F. Ramsey, Tennessee Love Ramsey, Bob Ramsey, Rose Reynolds Ramsey, Charlie Ramsey, Gordon Ramsey, Lina Ramsey.*

got into confusion and immediately retreated Crittenden conducted the retreat back to their breastworks[2] from which they were driven at three Oclock of the same day that night Crittenden with his forces crossed Cumberland River retreating toward Knoxville—it is reported and believed that Prices forces in Mo have whipped and captured about 10,000 of the enemy there is a report also but not believed that Confederate forces have whipped the Federal on the Potomac again in a late fight. The enemy under Crittenden have moved from Calhoun to Carrolton at which place they are in forty five or fifty miles of this place and ten or fifteen miles nearer than they were at Calhoun. When they began to move we thought we would have had a fight here before now but now there is no telling when it will take place but it is no doubt not far off—Burgess Modrell is in good health— Rob[t]. High has Mumps—Geo Blain is sick but missed his fever today Capt Moody has had Flux for near two weeks has been better at times but has finally gone to a private house—All of our company except those that are dead are doing tolerably well none of them are in any great danger as far as I am able to judge

I have had but few letters from home. Nothing more at present.

Yours in filial regard &c
C.W. Love

1. Privates were paid eleven dollars per month until June of 1864 when it increased to eighteen dollars.

2. A temporary fortification built up from the earth to breast height in order to provide protection.

Letter 24

{1862
{{Camp Washington February the 4th

Dear Sisters

I embrace the present opportunity of writing you few lines to inform you how we are still getting on and what our prospects are. ~~Bu~~ But I havent any news to write you except that Maj= Vandorn is our Maj= Gen= and commander= inchief. I only write you because I have an opportunity of sending it by hand to Dallass for there is nothing atall that will interest. John was a little Sick but is getting well in fact he was not much sick. he has been getting so fat that his horse can hardly carry him You can judge of his fat by the following figure.. 205.. lbs. Orders have just got into camps for all the soldiers to be that are out on furlough to be called in and no others to be granted except the cick furloughs. I have been to Vanburen Since I wrote to you last or [rather] While I was at

Charles Franklin Ramsey and Nancy Rebecca Farnsworth Ramsey, also known as Nannie. C.F. married Nannie after Tennessee's death in 1923. It was the second marriage for both.

VanB John Sent it off. And while I was there I had my pistol stold.. the circumstances are these .. I left it in a gunsmiths Shop to have a bead put on it and I told him my name and told him not to let anybody have it but me .. but had.nt been gone 20 minutes before it was missing .. he blamed it on a man that come there while he was working on another pistol While he at other times blamed it on another man from this Regt= I knew the last young man and I also knew that he did..nt get it and finally he Said that he thought I took it off and I made him take that back for if he had..nt I think I should have got on to him. but I mad him pay me $50 for it and fortunately bought another at $40 I told him that if he would get the pistol he could have his money back for it was Joe.^{s} but I believe he stold it himself and [Culm] is ~~t~~ trying to get it. I saw Mrs= [Culm] and Miss Laurea while I was at town and had a long talk with them.. they are both in good health .. especially Miss Laurea for she is [tho] rather fleshy. She enquired about all the girls and told her all I could. The health of the Regt is fine. Give my love to all the family to Cousin Sallie and [Vane] Foster and tell them to write to me. I would like to receiv a letter from cousin Sallie or Vane either. Give my love to Nannie Serena and Mollie .. and all other enquiring friends. Tea coppy this and Send it to ~~bett~~ Betty for I haven't time to write to her in a different letter and tell her to give my love to all the friends in F[1]= And tell Lou Aunt Mary and cousin Joe to write to me. I think I shall write to Mollie and Serena in a few days to let them know that I have not forgot them entirely. Tell father that I have not received a letter from him yet but I suppose you tell all that is necessary but I have not received but one from you yet one from Betty and one from Vanhorn. One of the principle objects in writing this is to tell you to Direct your letters as you will see on the small piece of paper[2] untill I tell you to direct them differently.

With these few hastily writen lines I remain Your brother, Sam.. B. Love. Joe P= sends his love to you and all other enquiring friends. There is nothing more that I can think but to write and tell every body else to write to me.

1. The letter suggests Tea resides in Fairfield at the time the letter was written.
2. The piece of paper Sam refers to is not preserved within the collection.

Letter 25

Cyrus was wounded during a breakout assault during the February 15 Battle of Fort Donelson. After a Confederate breakout attempt failed (partly because of an improbable blunder by Confederate brigadier general Gideon Pillow), the besieged Fort Donelson surrendered to Ulysses S. Grant on February 15, 1862; nearly 12,500 Confederates were captured. This Union victory at Donelson followed the seizure of Fort Henry. The capture of the two forts represented significant Union victories in the western theater that opened the Cumberland River for invasion into Tennessee. According to the historical record, Cyrus's report of enemy casualties at Fort Donelson appears to be off by a factor of ten.

Franklin Co Tenn
March the 15th 1862
John & Elizabeth Karner's:

Dear brother & Sister:

I have written to no one in smartly more than a Month — to day is one Month since I was wounded at Donaldson — I wrote or rather scribbled a letter to father and mother a day or two ago and it was mailed yesturday. I did not wish to write until I was able to say that I was improving — my wound is nearly well but the disease it caused in my liver lungs and body generally is not out of me yet and I am very weak. not able to walk but a few hundred yards at a time without rest I am improving though very fast and will no doubt by the favor of Providence be able to join the army in time for the next big fight which I believe from all appearances will be some where down on the Tenn River — I do not know at this time what part of the army I will join I think however at this time that I will join Col Wharton's Texas Cavalry[1] for the sake of being with Texans and more particularly to be with some persons that I know — but I do not know that I will do this as the Cavalry Service is much harder and not so effective in a fight as the infantry It is impossible to learn the truth here about anything: the last news I have from the enemy's forces at Nashville is that they were moving by degrees down the river I suppose the purpose is for Buel & Grant[2] to join their forces when they will have about One Hundred and forty Thousand with which they expect to move up the Tennessee River and whip every thing as they go — My opinion however is that they are in trap from which it will be hard for them to extricate themselves

The enemy no doubt are gloating over what they did at Ft Donaldson but they have no cause to glory if they would only admit the facts in the case we killed about 5000 or 6000 of them [?][3] their wounded are certainly in proportion to the killed we [also took][4] about 600 of them prisoners — they killed about 1000 or 1200 of us and wounded of us in proportion and then they captured the most of our little army which at first numbered only about 16000 or 17000 and we had no recruits after the fight begun — they had 31,000 to begin with they afterwards received first 10,000 at another time 15,000 recruits and I am of the opinion that they received a third reinforcement for the fight on Sunday on which day they captured our forces — I have understood that our men were taken to the barracks at Louisville Kentucky — I have not been able to get out from here to learn anything since I got here I have heard it reported and it seems to be confirmed that Price has had another big fight it seems from all that I can learn in Arkansas in which he whipped the enemy killing 7000 of them and had taken 10,000 prisoners and persued them 20 miles — that M^c^Intosh and another of our Generals had been killed but I have not been able to learn any of the particulars — I have not seen a News paper in more than a Month — you can therefore guess at my chances to learn anything.

I left Uncle Andrew and cousin John at Hopkinsville waiting on some eight or ten sick boys cousin Andrew was the sickest and I did not believe he would live nor do I think Uncle Andrew had any hopes of his living he had Pneumonia very bad in one lung and a slight touch of it the other I waited on him about four days before I left and I could see no change for good — but by the favor of Providence he may have got well I can only give my opinion of his condition when I saw him last. I think it altogether probable that they were made prisoners by the fellow Jackson of whom I have spoken before. I am going into the war again if God wills and I do not think I will take such traitors to their country as Jackson prisoner if I know it. Kentucky and East Tennessee are full of just such tories as he is and they deserve no Mercy

The reasons why I am here and not a prisoner with the other boys is just this. I was wounded about 11 O,[c] in the Morning (Saturday Morning the 15th Febr) and the wounded were all taken aboard of the boats to be taken to Nashville. the boats started up the river about sundown just as the fight began again in the evening — We were taken on up to Nashville where every thing was in great confusion Nashville having been given up to the enemy — We got to Nashville late Sunday night — in the morning the Surgeons told us that the wounded who were able to report themselves to R.R. conductors would get free passes to their homes until they got well — I took passport with a young man by the name of Rob[t] Grey expecting to go with him to his fathers down in Alabama but my wound had not been dressed at all and was doing badly so that I was compelled to stop at Tullahoma in this county and have it dressed. I then came here to Mr. Petty[s] 5 miles from Tullahoma where I have been treated as kindly as if I had had my pockets full of money of which I had none. until about two weeks ago a Dr. Ripito[5] agent for the State of Texas for the relief of soldiers gave me a $20 00. Confederate bond — Nothing more now I will write again when I join the army –

Yours &c.
CW Love

1. After his escape and convalescence, Cyrus joined the Eighth Texas Cavalry under John A. Wharton, not to be confused with Jack Wharton, a field officer in the Sixth Texas Cavalry. Wharton succeeded Terry as commander of the Eighth Texas Cavalry Regiment, but the unit retained the name Terry's Texas Rangers.

2. Probably Union general Don Carlos Buell and Ulysses S. Grant.
3. There is a water stain on the page that may conceal a word here.
4. A water stain partially obscures these words.
5. Dr. A.H. Rippetoe, from Brenham, Texas.

Letter 26

The following is a fragment in the Love family letters. The first two pages of what appears to be a four-page letter are absent, leaving the third and fourth pages, which are preserved here. The accompanying envelope, a rare occurrence in the collection, has been transcribed in order to provide the date, author, and addressee.

Estill Springs March 17/ 62 Paid 10c
Mr. Ja^{s} M Love
Springfield
Limestone Co
Texas

P.M.^{s} please hasten this to its destination

C.W. Love Capt. Moody^{s} Co[1]
Col Gregg^{s} Reg^{mt} Tex—Vo^{l}..

With a young friend of the Waco Rifles Reported myself his name is Robt Grey he and I started to his fathers down in Alabama but I was unable to go any farther than here—the house of Mr Ely Petty and his wife where I have been as kindly treated as I could desire for the four weeks that I have been here I have also had a Dr Harris attending on me for nothing but he has taken as good care of me as if he were going to get a regular fee—I have also been visited by a Dr. Ripito an agent for the State of Texas to distribute money to the needy Texan Soldiers he gave me $20.00 Confederate Note this is the first I have received since I left home and it was gladly recd as I had been entirely out for some time.

I will possibly not be able to leave here in a week or two yet as my ~~I~~ wound is not yet healed

Go back to next page

and do not know what Regmt I will join but I expect I will join Col Wharton^{s} Cavalry as it is the only Texas Reg^{mt} I know of any where about here I will write to you as soon as I locate myself if I should stop any length of time at any place I wish you to write to me but until I let you know that I am located for some time it will be useless to write I have delayed writing till now because I wanted to know that I was improving before I wrote

Yours with fillial regard
C.W. Love

P.S. I left uncle Andrew John W & Andrew jr at Hopkinsville I have not heard from them since but think it more than likely they were taken prisoners by Jackson

CWL

1. Written vertically on the left side of the envelope.

Letter 27

The following is a fragment in the Love family letters; based on Cyrus's account that General Buell "made a grand movement from Nashville twenty days ago," the earliest this letter could have been written is March 17, 1862. (Nashville was taken on February 25, 1862.) Sections of the letter were apparently torn from the remainder, leaving four disconnected strips, which are preserved here. These have been ordered according to context clues and probability so as to retain the presumed flow of the letter.

Dear parents:

This leaves me in tolerable good health but yet undetermined whether to join this (Co[l].. Whartons Reg or to go and join Stones Regmt so that I might be with Sam[l] & John if they are alive of which I am somewhat doubtful if they were in the fight when M[c]Culloch and M[c]Intosh were killed from all I can learn it was a severe fight and continue

The enemy they are also well armed and we have a good many cannon of all sorts of sizes—I am of the opinion that Genl Buel and Genl Grant have joined their forces and now have on the Tenn River about twenty miles north of where I am ^130.000 to 150.000 men^ at this time Grants forces came [?][1] River on One Hundred and Sixty transport boats of [?] kinds—Buels made a grand movement from Nashville [?] twenty days ago coming in this direction—they are

Tenn who act as spies and informers for the yankee army and thereby been the cause of a great many of our sick soldiers to be taken as well as a good many of the more prominent citizens—they got information at one place between Nashville and Murfresborough and went fifteen miles off the road to make a prominent Secessionist a prisoner and with him they got five sick soldiers—I as I have before told you was at old Mr Pettys about five miles from a little R. R. town by the name of Tulahoma—Six Hundred and eighty of the enemys cavalry came to that place and had been there nearly twenty four hours before I knew anything

I understand that Vandorn and Price will possibly be here with their forces to take part in the fight if so I will try to see the boys—I also hear that Siegel with about forty thousand of the enemy are at New Madrid and with the positions of our forces and the enemys there is no telling how mony of either side will be in the engagement—I have heard that we have strong batteries below the enemys transports if this is the case and they are supported by a strong force of cavalry and infantry there will be no chance for them to pass down the river to bring up more forces—I have also learned just a little

1. The page is torn here.

Letter 28

In this letter, Sam describes the Battle of Elkhorn Tavern (perhaps better known as the Battle of Pea Ridge) fought March 6-8, 1862, in Arkansas. Although the battle was a Confederate loss, and despite what Sam writes about him here, CSA major general Earl Van Dorn remained in good favor with the Confederate Congress, and wrote in his official report that "I was not defeated, but only foiled in my intentions." Both Sam and Cyrus write about Van Dorn in several of their letters. He was placed in command of the trans-Mississippi region by CSA president Jefferson Davis in early 1862. Cyrus describes Van Dorn's death in Letter 66.

{{Pleasant Hill Franklin Co Ark March the ^1862^ 30th

Dear Father & Mother

I write you these few lines more to let you know how to direct your letters than for any other purpose though I will tell you what little I have learned since I wrote my last. I will first speak of the late battle at the Elk horn tavern near the line of Mo= and Ark=. What I have learned is this

§ I learned it from a Lieut= Martin that was a prisoner in the hands of the Feds= at the time the battle was going on and saw it all. He was from our Regt.§ The Federal General had thrown up brest works across the telegraph road that was a mile long and expected the attack to be made in that direction but instead of taking that road our army took the Bentonvill road and turned the right flank of their breastworks and attacked them on the flank and in the rear Gen= Price going to the rear. While this was being done Gen= Seigel sent to Gen= Curtis for reinforcements and artillery but he would not send it for two hours believing that the attack in that quarter was only a feint to draw off his forces from the brestworks so that they could be taken by storm. Lieut Martin says that if on friday evening they had been attacked by all our force the last one of them could have been taken for Gen=Price was on one side of them and Gen Mcullough^{s} brigade was on the other and it is certain that if Gen Mcullough had not been killed the attack would have been made but as soon as Van Dorn heard of his death he {{Van Dorn}} was whipped and he was the only man in our ranks except Gen Pike that was ever whipped for all that were in it say that they were not whipped for the simple reason that they did not get to fire a gun. There was several thousand of our men that did not fire a gun.

General Van Dorn has lost the confidence of the army on account of the way he has acted in this first battle. The boys are all well or were well when I heard from them last. I took the flux a few days before the reg^{t}.. left and could not go with it but I am well now and expect to follow them tomorrow. They lef here this day week for Jackson port it is at the mout of Black River. I did not stay at winterquarters but I am two mills from there: at house where I have been treated as well it was possible. ~~Th~~ The lady is the kindest most motherly old lady I ever met. I have nothing more to write to you now So accept the filial regards of your son

Sam

Direct your letters to Jackson Port Ark

Letter 29

Corinth Miss
Apl 1st A.D. 1862
Jas M. & T.A. Loves:

Dear parents:

This leaves me in a still improving condition and at present with the boys from Limestone Co.... Sol Skruggs Wm & Jos Lynches and also Bulger Peoples Wm Perry and Mr Grant— Mr Thornton and in fact a good many of the Limestone boys with whom I had formerly but little acquaintance I find that there are at this place a numbr possibly as many as thirty of Col Greggs Regmt — three of them are of my company — men who have been sick most of the Winter– they are Mssrs Oliver. Steele. Cason — they and most of the others will get discharges today through Dr Alston W[?][1] now a member of Genl Clarks staff — the Dr is in good health– these three of the boys will be at home very soon as soon possibly as this gets to or possibly sooner as I may send this to you by Mr Steele– Terry Wylie is here also and is in good health he was sick and at Clarksville when the fight took place at Donaldson. I have learned from Mr Cason that Uncle Andrew and Several of the boys got away from Hopkinsville– Andrew died and cousin John was too sick to be moved I do not know where Uncle Andrew is and was unable to learn any-thing until I had got here– I was not well enough to leave the place from which I wrote you the last letter but I had to do that or be taken by the enemy who were in five miles of me and had been for eighteen hour before I learned they were there the consequence to me was a walk down the R.R. about twenty six or twenty eight miles which tired me so much that I have not got over it yet— I had to carry my knapsack weighing about twenty lbs — I had also to walk nearly the whole distance on the cross ties of the R.R.— I got here day before yesturday morning and as I was not able to do active service I felt very gloomy and bad at the prospect of being sent to any reg^{mt} regardless of the consequences to me but as good fortune had it I was but a little time in finding the boys with whom I am now staying — I have learned that John & Sam were in the Apothliohon fight but did not get hurt — but I am fearful they have suffered in the last fight down in Arkansas. but as I do not know that I could get an answer from you before I would have to leave here I suppose I must continue ignorant of [their fate][2] and hope that it has been the will of the Almighty to protect them — God only knows how long this war will continue but as long as it does continue– separated as we are there but little chance for us to know much about each other.

I have learned from men just from Texas that there are reported to be upwards of hundred of the enemys gun boats inside of the bar at the mouth of the Mississippi and that the troops on the other side of the river at N.O. had been immediately put over on this side — they bring also the news that all of the troops on our coast had been ordered to Missouri and that new troops were being raised to supply their places. I learn that there was some skirmishing between our troops and the enemy as ourforces were falling back in Virginia in which we had the advantage — in one case about 300 of our forces whipped about 500 of the enemy six of our men were killed and upwards of one hundred wounded — 40 of the enemy were killed and 100 prisoners taken the enemy^{s} wounded were considerable but the number was not known– Our forces burned all the bridges on the R. Roads down to their present position which is said to be a much better one than that formerly occupied. the bridges all along down from from Nashville to the Cumberland Gap have also been burnt. There will no doubt be a tremendous fight near here in a few days the Texas Rangers were out on a scout day before yesturday and got back yesturday they saw some movements on the part of the enemy but do not know they were advancing this way but [suppose][3] they were the heard cannon firing all day [yesturday][4] which the thought were from the enemys gun[boats][5] — I myself heard a cannon two or three times yesturday evening about dark and took them to be cannon of a land battery if so the enemy are in a few miles of us or were when the cannon were fired– let all this be as it may there is no doubt we are on the point of fighting a great battle– I have just heard that Co[l] Mores Regiment from near Galveston got here this morning and passed on to the East of town– Merchants all through this country are charging the most enormous prices for every thing a 75[ct] knife for $2.00 [Soap] $1.00 pr lb small letter paper such as sold for about .30[cts] in Texas $100 pr Qr. Cotton Cards[6] at $6.00 to $9.00 a pr — the people ought to remember as soon as the war is over.

Yours in filial Regard &c
C W Love

N.B. written on my knees —

1. A horizontal tear in the page obscures this word.
2. There is a hole in the paper here.
3. The page is torn here.
4. There is a hole in the page here.
5. There is a hole in the page here.
6. Possibly cords as in corduroy pants.

Letter 30

As predicted in the previous letter, Cyrus was a part of a "tremendous fight" in southwestern Tennessee on April 6-7, 1862. Known as the Battle of Shiloh, it was the bloodiest battle on American soil up to that point and was a significant Union victory. While Sam and John were not directly involved, as evidenced by the following letter, their regiment subsequently moved toward Corinth, in northern Mississippi, near the Shiloh battlefield.

Memphis Aprile the 26 ^7^{th}^ 1862

Dear Father and Mother

As we have halted this evening to await further orders, ^I thought I would write you a few hasty lines^ We are in 3 miles of Corinth and it will be but a few days till we will be engaged for Gen= Beauregard Sent 80..000 men forward yesterday and w ^we^ are listening every hour to hear the battle begin. We are at present 20 miles from Shiloh where the last battle was fought and we all feel that almost our all depends upon the issue: we also ~~feel~~ have perfect confidence in our ability to whip them whenever we ~~maet~~ meet them on land and notwithstanding we have been so unfortunate in loosing our forts on the Miss= River and the sea cost we have not at all Despaired of ultimate success for it is the opinion of all that when this battle is fought: that if we whip {{and there is but little doubt of it}} the Fed^{s}= will have to give up all the places they have taken. There is but little Doubt about our success although the Fed^{s}= have near 200..000 while we have only 150.000. We heard the guns at Memphis while they were shelling fort Pillow a distance of 40 miles. I have not heard anything of Cy uncle John or any of our relations.

I believe it is the determination of all to fight them as long as there is any of us living so that if they get it they will get a Depopulated country. There is not any news that I could write that you would not hear before you would get this. In fact I doubt very much about this ever getting to you. There is one thing that I wish to say. It is this the people of Texas as well as all the other States ought to prepare for the worst or in other words they ought to organize into companies and $Regt^{s}$ one and all for the purpose of repelling an invasion for I believe it is the polacy of the Northern Government to take possession of all the Southern States and they by doing so will possibly weaken these forces so much that <u>we</u> can invade. but to prevent them from getting entire possession it would be well to be prepared to receiv them at home. I have nothing more to write only We are all well and I do sincerely hope that these few lines will find you all enjoying the same blessing. Give my love to all enquiring friends and more espetially to the family and relations.

With these few hastily and lastly written lines I remain your Son

S.. B. Love

Letter 31

This letter is unique in the collection, featuring a postal seal on the upper left-hand corner.

Rienzi
Apl 28th A.D. 1862
Jas M. & T.A. Loves:

Dear parents:

I have concluded to write again not knowing whether it will reach you or not but hope it may as all of you would like to from us often. I would like very much to hear from you but it is possibly best for you not to undertake to answer as yet there is no certainty that the place to which your letters might be directed would be in the hands of the enemy. There have been various reports of fighting we have had the report here that two gun boats of the enemy had passed fort Jackson and were shelling the city of N.O. but a man in camp just from N.O. says it is not so— he says he had not got more than to the third station from N.O. till he heard the report that a telegraphic dispatch announced the passing of the boats and shelling the city— there is a report just in camp that we[1]

fifteen iron clad boats at N.O. but how true this is I cannot say—There will no doubt be a tremendous fight here in a few days the enemy are coming this way from the Shilo battle ground in great numbers. the report has just got here that they had the N.O. Crescent Regmt who were

Rien:

Apl 28th A.D. 1862

Jas. M. & T. A. Love:

Dear parents!

I have concluded to write again not knowing whether it will reach you or not but hope it may as all of you would like to from us often. I would like very much to hear from you but it is possibly best for you not to undertake to answer as yet there is no certainty that the place to which your letters might be directed would be in the hands of the enemy. there have been various reports of fighting we have had the report here ~~that two gun boats of the enemy had passed fort~~ Jackson and were shelling the city of N. O. but a man in camp just from N. O. Says it is not So — he Says he had not got more than to the third Station from N. O. till he heard the report that a telegraphic dispatch announced the passing of the boats and Shelling the city — there is a report just in camp that we

Letter 31, written by Cyrus in April of 1862, bears a postal seal. Special Collections, Mary Couts Burnett Library, Texas Christian University.

fifteen iron clad boats at N.O. but how
true this is I cannot Say— There will no
doubt be a tremendous fight here in a
few days the enemy are coming this
way from the Shilo battle ground in great
numbers. the report has just got here that
they had the N.O. Crescent Regmt who were
near the enemy watching them and that
they were Surrounded and it took them
two days to get out it is no doubt the inten
tion of our Genls to draw the enemy as far
from the river as they can and when the
next fight comes on I feel confident
we will whip them badly— we have a
report here that there has been Severe fighting
at Ft Pillow in which the enemy were
driven back— The enemy are in considerable
force on the R.R. from here to Huntsville
Ala— they are committing a great many
outrages on citizens as they com this way

Letter 31, extant page 2.

Some of their pickets killed Mrs Highs
brother— they have taken old general Garth
and Mrs Gregg prisoners and destroyed
a great deal of property about Genl. Garths
house— I have just heard that Jones Regmt
is here near Corinth in twelve or thirteen
miles of where I now am but I will not
be able to see the boys if they are there
as this regmt is ordered to be ready to march
at a moments warning and is also to move
to Russelville Ala tomorrow— I will see
them if God spares us as soon as I can
No news of importance more than the above

Yours in filial regard

C.M. Love

Letter 31, page 3.

near the enemy watching them and that they were surrounded and it took them two days to get out it is no doubt the intention of our Gen[l] to draw the enemy as far from the river as they can and when the next fight comes on I feel confident we will whip them badly—we have a report here that there has been severe fighting at Ft. Pillow in which the enemy were driven back—The enemy are in considerable force on the R.R. from here to Huntsville Ala— they are committing a great many outrages on citizens as they com this way some of their pickets killed Mrs Highs brother—they have taken old general Garth and [Majs] Gregg prisoners and destroyed a great deal of property about Genl Garths house—I have just heard that Stones Reg[mt] is here near Corinth in twelve or thirteen miles of where I now am but I will not be able to see the boys if they are there as this regmt is ordered to be ready to march at a moments warning and is also to move to Russelville Ala tomorrow—I will see them if God spares us as soon as I can No news here of importance more than the above

Yours in filial regard
C.W. Love

1. There is at least one missing page in between this line and the next.

Letter 32

Corinth Miss=May the 11th 1862

Dear Sister[1]

I embrace the present opportunity of writing you a few lines to let you know how we are getting on also to inform you of the prospect of a batle here also to tell of a small battle between some 10..000 of the Federal and about 5..000 of our troops though there was near 25..000 of us on the field but we all did not get into the fight and had it not been for a misfortune in getting courier ^killed ^ that was sent to Gen=Price with orders to cut them off from the bridge across a large creek that was in their rear we would have bagged the whole arrangement. but as it was they got away by doing some responsible running though they did not run until they had tried to take one of our batteries but in making the attempt they caught thunder their cavalry and infantry both.

I will here state that I was there but did not get into the fight. I will also State that I never saw a cooler set of men in my life there was not the least excitement although we were expecting to be in the affray every minute The fact is every one was surprised at himself for we all expected to be more or less excited before we got into it. We drove them about two miles and burnt their Bridge and took down their telegraph wire It would be impossible for me to give the number killed or wounded on either side though I saw three dead men of 2 them were Feds and one of ours one of the fe Feds had his head shot off. We captured several prisoners and some of their artilery the fight took place on the 9th. We have heard since that they have crossed the creek and come to Farmingto a little town four miles from our intrenchments.

It will not be many days before the battle comes off and we intend to give them one of the most complet thrashings they ever got. We have about 125..000 and the Feds 150.000 Soldiers here so you will see that we are nearer equal than we have ever been since the war began. The forces at Shiloah was 32000 against 75000 the Federal loss killed wounded and missing was 13..000 and our 6000.[2] I have at last heard of Cy and Andrew Cy was wounded at Donaldson but is well and belongs ^to^ Col.. Whartons {Terrys old} Regt but Andrew is dead though I expect you have heard of them before I did. I intend to try to get a transfer to that Regt for myself and John. I saw John [Menes] who first told me about him and I saw Griffin Kenady who told me that he was in his company. I will have to close this letter. The boys are all ^well^ except John Sharp and there is nothing serious the mater with him. We reorganised today and elected our field and company officers We are in for two years longer if the war does not terminate sooner. I did intend to come home this coming winter but the conscript law will not allow any one to leave So we all w^i^ntered again and I reckon it is well enough that the act was past and become a law. The worst feature that I see in it is this..it is a tyrannical law and is consequently a bad precedent but I think the necessities of the cause required that something should be Done. It is the opinion of almost every body that the war will not last longer than this year but I donot think it will be closed until after two hard battles are fought one in Va and the other in Miss=. They will have to leave N..O.. this summer or the yellow fever will kill them all.

It is reported here that the members to Congress from the western States have resigned and say they will not go back until this war is Settled. The cause of it was Lincolns Abolition message to Congress.[3] I do.not believe it. I am in good health Give my love to all the family and relations and to all enquiring friends and to yourself a brothers love. S..B..Love. May the 13th

We will leave camp this evening but I do not know where we are going though~~t~~ it is thought that we are going to attack the enemy. It is reported that the Tenn= River has fallen so that the Fed=Gun Boats have had to go down the River and if it is true Gen Beauregard knows it and I expect that if they are gone so that they cannot ~~attack~~ protect them it is more than likely that the attack will be made tomorrow

1. Based on the content in comparison with previous letters, this letter was likely sent to Tea.

2. Whether intentionally or from misinformation, Sam's figures are incorrect. Federal forces actually numbered 65,000 against 45,000 Confederates, and Confederate casualties were 10,500 rather than the 6,000 Sam cites in the letter.

3. Likely the Compensated Emancipation Act of April 16, 1862, which eliminated slavery in Washington, DC.

Letter 33

This letter is written in severely faded pencil, and is one of the most difficult to read in the collection. Evidently the first letter composed by Sam was not immediately sent, and appears to be opened and appended by John Love a few weeks before being mailed to Tea.

Near Baldwin Miss June the 5th [1862]

Dear Sister

As I have met with another opportunity of writing a few hasty lines for the purpose of informing you of what has h happened since my last. We have retreated from Corinth about 30m and we are going to go 15 m farther. We retreated day and night for 3 days We had some tolerably heavy ~~fig~~ Skirmishings for 3 or 4 days before we commenced retreating.. the enemy throwing a great many shells at us but they did not hurt anybody. Our batteries Silenced theirs every time time they planted them. I cannot describe the retreat.. there was a great deal of suffering and a good many of the sick died on account of the fatigue. I will have to close. I am well Jasper [Bowden] and B Kenady are at the hospital Pete is waiting on them Joe [Prender]= is still unwell though there is nothing very serious the matter with him I think I have not heard of John but once since he left. Neither have I heard of Cy—I have not received a letter from home in 3 months. Hoping these few lines will find you all enjoying good health I remain your affectionate brother

S..B.. Love

Tylor June 25th 1862

Tea I broke open this letter & read it we are all in good health so far as know—all of our co [?][1] boys. are good.. we are now ordered to Clarksville will start there in a few days. I have nothing more to write the fact is there is nothing to write

so nothing more from your brother, John—

1. Illegible mark, struck through.

Letter 34

Camp near Chatanooga Tenn
June 14th 1862
Jas M & T.A. Loves:

Dear parents:

After a long delay I have an opportunity to give you Some information of my whereabouts and condition= We were started from Corinth about 6 or 7 weeks ago and came up to Lambs ferry where Scotts cavalry had just had a brush with some of the enemy near Athens on or near Elk river — they became after a while too strong for him and compelled him to recross both the Elk and Tennessee= when we got to the ferry (on the Tennessee) it took us about two [days][1] to cross our forces and wagons after crossing Some four or five hundred of our Regmt & the Kentucky 1st Regmt went on a Scout and killed and made prisoners of 69 of the enemy at a place on Elk River about thirty miles from where we crossed the Tenn a few days afterward the most of the Ky 1st & our Regmt (the 1st Texas Rangers or 8th Texas Cavalry) went an=other Scout up Elk River and were cut off from our wagons by about 4000 of the enemys forces consisting in part of infantry & part cavalry— We started immediately toward Winchester Tenn picking up their couriers and Spies as we went until we got to Winchester we lay about that place a few days when we learned that some 1500 or 1800 of the enemy had come from Huntsville on the hunt for us we starte about day light with the intention of surprising them but had not gone far when we larned that they after marching a good part of the night were at Winchester we turned about and returned toward winchester but were going in South of town when the enemy discovered us and shot a few Shells at us doing however but very little harm — We returned to our camp and Scouted about the town for some days and finally about 250 of us in making a Scout concluded to attack the town or rather the enemy that were in it in the charge we were in view of town for more than half a mile — we caught 7 of their pickets in about 200 yds of the public Square and charged on till the front of the Column who were Kentuckyans and a few Rangers were up in the Square one of the Ky^{s} was killed and 3 or 4 wounded one of them mortally there was but little firing done when we retreated as we at first intended we do not know whether we killed [any][2] of them or not Someone said three were killed on the bridge as we were going in — another fellow said he saw one lying under the bridge but I Saw none there — it was also said that Some of them were killed in the Court house but there is no way of knowing the truth about it unless the enemy tell it themselves which they are not likely to do as they reported that they had killed 36 of us which they knew to be false in as much as they could not have known that they had killed but one of us — we camped that night in about 6 miles of them — they were so badly Scared that they threatened to kill the people of the town if they were attacked that night — they Started during the night at double quick for Huntsville 45 miles distant ^where they arrived^ before night of that day — We passed back throug the town next day and returned to our old camping place with the view of crossing the mountains to Chatanooga We crossed the Mountains the next day into Sequochey[3] valley and the next day we crossed the Tenn River Genl Adams with the Ky Reg^{mt} Remaining in the valley — in a few days a force of 4000 or 5000 of the enemy came very near surprising the Ky^{s} having crossed the Mountains behind us a Strong force came up from Huntsville between the River and the Mountains with the intention no doubt of hemming us up in this valley and they would possibly have hemmed the Kys if we had not been watching them from this side of the river — We sent a few balls from Some of our cannon at them and our boys were frequently giving them a taste of Enfield and Sharpsrifle balls[4] — from appearances they got in a notion it was not good policy to show themselves very much where our boys had a chance to Shoot at them — they however would get behind Shelter and fire back at us very frequently but did no damage at all whether our boys hit any of them is not known a part of their forces came up opposite Chatanooga and Shelled the town a couple of days but did but little harm wounding only one or two men and injuring a few houses to the amount of about fifty dollars worth — no one knows what harm we did them — it is reported in camp though that somebody went over after the enemy left and found three graves in two of which there were 15 men one of whom was thought to be a field officer and in the third two cannon that had been dismounted by our guns — this may or may not be true — The enemy are reported by a courier of this morning to be coming up the river again — I do not feel warranted in writing about all that I know is going on but feel certain from what I have learned that our Officers are well informed of the enemys intentions — It is but few times now that we can get any information from us to you. S.B.L. sent me his pistol — I learned also that J.W.L. had gone with the horses — Sam was well about two or three weeks ago when the balance of the regmt left for this place — I understand that Sam & John will if they are permitted ^to live^ until they can do so get transfers and join this Reg^{mt} — I hope they may be able to do so I do not know but suppose Ja^{s}[5] is with Tyus in Arkansas. I guess it is almost impossible for us all to get together — but I hope the Almighty will Save our lives through this war until the Southern Confederacy is fully established and at peace with all the other nations of the world on good and honorable terms and let us all meet together with you again Yet if it is the will of the Deity that we Should die in defence of our cause I hope we may be permitted to meet again beyond the confines of time I do not expect to go back to Texas until this war ends in a recognition of our government by the Northern government

May the God of heaven bless and protect us from Spiritual evils

Yours in filial regard
C W Love

P.S.
I am well — the Regmt is in good health and all have been in remarkably good health since we left Corinth

Yours &c
C.W.L.

1. There is a hole in the paper here.

2. There is a hole in the paper here.

3. Sequatchie Valley, Tennessee.

4. The Enfield musket rifle was a popular muzzle-loading, one-shot musket and was the most widely used weapon of the Confederates during the Civil War. The Model 1859 Sharps rifle was a single-shot breechloader; not many were produced, as they were expensive to manufacture, and most of the ones used in the war were issued to sharpshooters.

5. Most likely James Love.

Letter 35

Camp Maurey June the 17th 1862

Dear Sister[1]

as I have another opportunity of Sending a letter to Tx by hand I make the best use of my opportunity I can. There is not any news of importance here now. The Feds are not following us from Corinth nor is it believed that they will. Gen= Stonewall Jackson has whipped the Yanks under Banks in Va worse than they were ever whipped before and drove them back in to Meryland also 20,000 of our troops befor Richmond drove 50,000 of the Feds out of their intrenchments and back into the Chickahominy River Swamp killing wounding and taking a great many prisoners also a good quantity of military stores. We are here Drilling and eating and waiting for the Feds to come on to us though they will not do it. Why they will not follow us I can^no^t tell though it is believed that they are afraid to come any farther down.= Their Soldiers are dying very rapidly. I shall have to make this letter very short as the man that is to carry it is going to start soon.

There is something going on here that is working for the worse or better but we cannot tell what it is. Old Abe undertook to open the ports of Norfolk N..O.. and other ports to Yankey merchants but the French and English Consuls would not let them put off anything observing at the same time that if he {{old Abe}} could not make the blockade effectual that their respective governments would help him ... the meaning of the remark was this that if the bockade was not raised for all neutral powers the yanks should not trade there either. There is no telling what will turn up in the course of three or four weeks.

I hope that the result of what is going on will result in peace.. There is a great many here that [confently] think that peace is not long off. It is reported {{and not without some chances of truth}} that Gen^s^ Beauregard Breckenrage and Price have gone to Richmond. }{

I shall now close by telling you of the health of the boys. First Jasper Bowden and Ben Kenady went to the hospital from Corinth Jasper was tolerably sick with the measles Ben was not very sick Pete went with them as a nurse he also was a little puny. Joe P= was sent to Lauderdale Spring[2] he was tolerably sick when he left thoug I have heard from him since he left.. he was getting better and I am looking for him every day. I am in good health and all the other boys are.

With these few hastily written lines I remain your brother S..B.. Love.

Give my love to all the family an connexion and all enquiring friends. Yours in haste.

N.B. I have just learned that the governments of England France and Spain have made Six propositions to the two governments for peace all of which the C..S.. are willing to accede to

I hope and believe it is true

Direct your letters to Jackson Miss

1. Most likely sent to Tea, or perhaps to Bettie.

2. A Confederate hospital located in east-central Mississippi, near the Alabama border.

Letter 36

In the following letter Cyrus describes some of the action of the Union's spring 1862 Peninsula Campaign, in which General George B. McClellan's massive Army of the Potomac slowly moved up the Virginia peninsula intending to lay siege to the CSA capital in Richmond. The Union army's incursion was finally halted in June when the newly-appointed commander of the Confederate forces, Robert E. Lee, commenced a bloody offensive in what became known as the Seven Days Battles. Richmond, for the time being, was saved.

Chatanooga Tenn..
June 29th 1862
Ja^s M & TA Loves:

Dear parents:

In a former letter I gave you the history of our travels from Corinth up through Tenn to this place. We have had no fighting since we have been here except some exchanges of shots across the River at this place and at various other places along down the river for about fifty miles below here. There has been some skirmishing near Knoxville in which our troops are said to have gained the advantage: but the most important news we have had up to this time of what is taking place in our favor is that after heavy skirmishing for several days there has been a general battle at Richmond Va in which the northern troops were completely routed that our troops had persued them to or across the Shenandoa River and had up to yesturday taken twenty thousand prisoners and ninety pieces of cannon and were still persueing and that the enemy were destroying all their munitions as they went. the above report comes to to us as having been telegraphe from Richmond to the Commander at this post (Genl Ledbetter) there is a possibility that the Northern Government will now accede to terms of peace if they do there will not be much more fighting but if they do not there is likely to be some hard fighting in Tenn= shortly as a considerable part of the enemy forces that were at Corinth are moving in that direction. There are about 15000 of them on the other side of the river about thirty miles below this place it was reported a few days ago that the enemy in strong force were coming up across the mountains on the other side of the River possibly with the view of effecting something against this place but more probably to form a junction with some of their forces from else where to act against Knoxville if they were there atall—we however crossed the river with a Scouting party the other day and went down to where they were said to be passing and found no sign of them they may have gone by some other road as they evidently design to do something in East Tennessee before long The report from Virginia is that 20.000 of the enemy were taken prisoners 90 pieces of cannon, about 140.000 stands of small arms and great quantities of munitions of war

If the enemys forces that are near this place conclude to fight us here in these mountains I have but little that we will whip them in fact if they undertake to stay here and their forces have badly whipped in Va it will be but a short time till we can have forces in their rear so as to capture the whole of them We still continue to have accounts of vessels getting through the blockade with valuable cargoes for sale two have got in within the last few days the first in Charleston harbor with 50 000 stands of arms and many other valuable articles—the other at Willmington N. C. which run aground and was fired on by the blockading fleet the guns of our batteries drove the fleet back and it is thought the most of its cargo will be saved it is reported to have had 1000 tons of powder and a good many arms on board the guns of our battery it seems fired on our own vessel so as to wet the powder and keep the enemys Shells from blowing her up—I have hear nothing from the boys since about a month ago they were well then or at least Sam was and as John went back with the horses when the Regmt. was dismounted. I suppose you know more about his health than I—there are a great many Unionists in the mountains of Tenn and a good many of them have joined the Federal army—I understand the Legislature of Missouri has refused to accept the Presidents (Lincolns) emancipation propositions

There are none of the Limestone boys dead—Walter Wood has putrid sore throat and has been very bad off but is better at this time—I have been blessed with entirely good health since I got well of my wound

Tell Robert to kiss Tenny for me. I would like to see you all but will not leave here till the war is over

Still hoping that we may all meet again I remain

Yours in filial regard &c.
C.W. Love

Letter 37

Itawambi Co Near Tupelo M[ss] July the[1] ^1862^

Dear Sister

~~ter.. not because~~ {{ I write this letter.. not because I think it will ever get to you but I think it is my duty to write and risk the desperate chances. Tea there is but little news to write. You have heard all about the Richmond battle before now and it is useless for me to write anything about it and there is but little else to write about. We have been having review all this week we first had a review of our Brigade then of the Devision[2] and last the army of the west.[3] The first was by gen Maurey the next by Gen Price and the last by Gen Bragg. As you know but little about it I will endevor to describe the movements of an army on review. In the first place they get a large open place about 2 miles long and ¼ of a mile wide they then form by devisions 4 brigades of about 3,000 each making a devision one devision behind an other each devision reaching the the lenght of the parade ground. The Maj.. Gen then ^gives^ the order rear open order march the rear rank stepping back 4 paces. The Gen.. reviewing {{ Sitting on his horse 150 paces in front of the center }} rides at a double quick to the right of the devis^ion^ then passes in front.. about 20 p^a^ces from the front rank the officers and men Saluting as he passes.. he then passes by the rear in the same manner as the front at a double quick until he gets back to the right passing around the right and back to the center again where he takes his position the command is then given by companies right wheel when all the companies whell to the right at the same time the command is then given to march {{ The artilery of each brigade marching in the rear of their respective Brigade }} when all the ~~the~~ bands commence playing the soldiers marching to the time until they pass the Gen. When each Brigade marches to their quarters.

It is a very interesting view to a spectator thoug not so much so to a soldier. The Feds have been bombarding Vicksburg till they have nearly destroyed it though they are no nearer taking ^it^ than they were at first. Only a few day since the little C.. S.. ram Arkansaw come through their Squdron of 30 gun boats sinking two of them as she was passing. She passed through one of the most terrific fires that was ever known though it did but little damage besides knocking off the stack chimney causing the crew to open one of their port holes to keep from smothering with the steam and smoke when a bomb entered the boat and exploded killing 6 and wounding 15 men though it done but little other damage. The citizens have left the city to get out of the way of the bombs.

I have not heard of but one person being killed and that was a benevolent old lady.. She was killed by a shell exploding.

The Federal fleet is still lying before Mobile.

They {the Feds} have been defeated on every ocasion this Spring & Summer and our cavalry keep poking it to them up in Tenn=.

The Fed^s^ have lost on the battlefield and in their hospital from 250.000 to 300 000 men while we have lost from 100.000 to 100 250. The health of an army was never better than that of the army of the West. My health was never better than it is now. So are all the rest of the Limestone boys Joe P= is not strong yet though he is well and gaining strength. I have not heard of John since he left.

Cy is up in Tenn with our cavalry force they have heard killed ^and wounded a great many^ and taken a good many prisoners.

I hear from him a few days since.. he was well. I sent him my six shooter from Corinth by Griffin H Kenady.

When John gets back I am going to try to get a transfer to the Reg^t^ he ^Cy^ is in.

I do not know when we will leave here nor do I have any idea which way we..ll go though most likely we will go north.. The general opinion three or four weeks ago was that France England and Spain would have an armed intervention but every one has given out the idea of intervention or even recognition by those governments. There is now no hope for peace until one or the other of the governments is entirely exhausted in both means ^men^ and means. The Fed^{s} are raising 300..000 more men to carry on the war. So you may not expect peace soon or at least until three or four big battles are faught one or two of them will likely be faught the comeing fall and wi^n^ter the others next Spring. I intend to try to get a furlough this Winter.. if I succeed I will come home if it.s only to stay a week. There is one great difficulty to be overcome befor a peace can be braught about if the North would a^c^knowledge the independence of the C.. S... it is the boundary question for the North will always want Meryland Kentucky and Misouri and the South will never give them up.

Tea I want you to write me a long letter when you get this {{ I have learned since I commenced writing that I can send it to Dallass by hand }} and tell me all about what is going on at home what all the people are doing what new improvements have been mad since I left and particularly about the things about home how the sheep horses and cows are getting on.. how the farm looks what for crop of corn, wheat oats rye and Hungarian grass.. If Father has made any improvements write Sam about every thing you can think of no matter how trifling it may be to you it will be of interest to me for there is nothi that comes frm hom that would not be of interest to me e^s^pecially as I have not heard a word from home since the 8th of Aprile.

Tea I have nothig eles to write about so I will have to close this letter. Tell Fannie Bettie ~~and all the~~ Eellen and all the connexion that because I do not write them it is no evidence that I have forgotten them. I cannot write to them all but I wish you would contrive to let them know where I am and how I am getting on and tell them to write to me. They cant imagin the pleasure it gives a soldier in camps to receive letters from friends at home.

I will now close give my love to all the family and all enquiring friends.

With this I remain your brother Sam..

P..S.. Tell Serena that I have found the nedle case that she gave me to be very useful. Send word to Joe^{s} people how he is getting on and tell them that he would have written but he ~~bu~~ burnt his hand the other day and cannot write now

S B Love

1. No day is provided here, but there is a space where it should go. Sam corrects his omission in Letter 38, telling Tea he wrote the letter above on the 27th of July, 1862.

2. A brigade generally consisted of four to six regiments; a division is the second largest unit of theoretically twelve thousand men.

3. Active from March 4, 1862 to September 28, 1862, the Army of the West consisted of about twenty thousand men and was later merged into the Department of Mississippi and East Louisiana.

Letter 38

After the Union took Corinth, Mississippi, on May 29, 1862, the principal bodies fought small skirmishes for most of the summer until Cyrus and the Army of Mississippi, otherwise known as the Army of the West under General Braxton Bragg, pushed north into Kentucky beginning July 21, 1862. Sam and John remained in Mississippi under Earl Van Dorn as part of a rearguard distraction tactic against General Grant.

This letter is incomplete: at least a page, including the signature, is missing. Given the fact that he fills in the date of the previous signed letter, in addition to the point of origin, handwriting, and the mention of Cy and John in the letter, the author is doubtless Sam. An undated postscript, signed by Sam, has been labeled and placed with the letter. In the postscript, Sam mentions events from earlier in the year, as well as news of the death of Jasper Bowden. Sam wrote about

Jasper being sick and in the hospital in Letters 33 and 35.

Itawamie Co.. near Pricevill MSS..
{August the 2nd 1862

Dear Sister[1]

As I have another opportunity of sending another letter to Waco by hand I thought I would make use of it though there is nothing more to write about now than there was then though it will be of some interest to you all to hear from me as often as possible.

I wish I had something to write about for it is a task to me to write when I have a great deal..but it ^is^ a much harder one when I have got nothing to write it is a much harder task.

There is possibly a few ~~lines~~ things that I did not write before that might be of some interest to you it is the enormous prices that every thing ~~demands~~ demands here.. especially anything that is to eat. For istance a chicken {{when it is to be had}} is from 50cts to $1.00 roasting eres[2] 25 to 50cts pr..Doz Apples and peaches $2 to 3 pr bu..[3].. butter mi^l^k and eggs cannot be had for love or money and everything in accordance with the above.. if you get meals vituals of bacon and bread it is 50cts.

I have not heard any thing from Cy since I wrote my last though I have heard from Col Morgan.s command several times they were still taking towns in Tenn.. and Ky. The reports that come in from them say that they are doing a great deal and loosing very few men. They have taken 1300 prisoners Gen.. Crittendon and Several Colonels among them and destroyed $1.000.000 of government property.[4] I intend to try to get a transfer to ~~Whath~~ Wharton[s] Regt as soon as John gets back and if I cannot do that I will try to get a discharge for John for it is impossible for him to serve as Infantry.

I have not got anything to write about so I will have to close this letter. The last letter I wrote to you was not dated.. it was written on the 27th of July. I also forgot to tell you how to direct your letters. And still another thing I forgot to tell you was that every body gets letters but me I do.nt know the reason. Though it looks like you had all forgot to write. Tell all the relations to write to me for it is the only real pleasure I have and even that pleasure comes very seldom for as I said in my last the last letter I received was written ~~of~~ ^on^ the 8th of April Near 4 months since. I really can..nt help thinking that you have written more than I have received but Fannie Betty and Eellen might write as well as others of my relations and friends ~~do~~ and I by writing to you might keep them all posted or if I can get ink and paper I will answer them all seperately.

[undated postscript]

P..S.. I was very glad to hear that Grand Father was getting better I have some hope now that I will get to see him again though from the tone of your letters when I was at winter quarters I expected the next letter to hear of his death. The boy that are not dead are all well. Jasper Bowden is dead he died with the Measles Pete has got back to camps fat and hearty. Ben ~~K~~ Kenady was getting well the last time I heard from him.

I knew all about Cy being wounded and Andrews death before I received your letter. Cy is in Wharton's Regt... Pete sends his respects to you

I have nothing more to write

Sam=

1. Most likely Tea.

2. Ears of corn.

3. Bushel.

4. According to historical accounts, Sam is correct; Union general Thomas Turpin Crittenden was captured by Nathan Bedford Forrest on July 13, 1862 during the First Battle of Murfreesboro.

Letter 39

At Camp near the junction of Tenn & Clynch
^River[1] below^ Kingston Tenn
Aug 8th 1862
Jas M & TA Loves:

Dear parents:

It has been a good while since you have heard from me—I now send you this letter by a man going to Texas hoping that when it reaches you—you will all be in as good health as I am—We are just from Middle Tenn where we went from Chattanooga—the first dash we made at the enemy was at Murfresboro—we killed wounded and captured about fifteen hundred of them two to four pieces of artillery fifteen hundred stand small arms a small quantity of army stores and burned about $4000.000 worth of commissary store and also 30 or 40 wagons and about 100 horses and mules—about a week after this went up in about four miles of Nashville and turned south to the rail Road burned three bridges and captured about one hundred men and thir arms—a unionist caused us to miss capturing about two hundred and fifty cavalry at Lebanon. Our horses are badly worn down and we are here to rest them a little we will no doubt be in active service soon—we learned yesturday that our forces about 15.000 strong had whipped about the same number of the enemy in an engagement at Cumberland Gap The Limestone boys that are here are all well and the health of Regiment generally is good. Terry Wylie was left at Chattanooga he was well when we left—I think that by the help of Providence we will soon have the enemy driven out of Tenn. Ky. & Va—I hope the war will close soon so that we may come home—We must stay as long as it lasts—this is my intention at least—I have learned that four Iron clad war Steamers have come into Mobile from Europe and that they are preparing Iron clad merchant vessels in Europe for Southern ports—I have heard nothing from Sam John & Joe Bake since I left Chattanooga East Tenn is almost as strongly union as any of the Northern States—[this] county sent 1700 men to the northern army and the town of Kingston sent two colonels to our enemy

There are numbers of bush whackers[2] all through these mountains who are shooting every Southern man they can as they pass the roads our men get some of them now and then—I learn that when the prisoners taken at Murfresboro were brought through Kingston the women of that place cried at the sight of our enemy^{s} misfortunes—nearly all the men of that place are in the northern army

There is a man here just from Ky.. he says since Morgans raid into that state the yankees are oppressing the people very much—I think we should not go into any part of the country where we are not able to hold the country

I expect you know the war news from every where better than I can Tell you—you cannot get any word to me but I will let you know where I am and how I am getting along evry opportunity—when you hear from me next I may be in Col Greggs Regmt again Yours in filial regard

C.W. Love

1. Clinch River.
2. Nonuniformed guerilla soldiers, usually union partisans.

Letter 40

Tupelo Aug.. the 11th 1862

Dear Sister

I embrace the present opportunity of writing to you to tell you the best news that I have had the p^l^easure of writing for some time it is this. Gen.. Price has given Co^{l}.. Ross permission to mount this reg^{t}.. again if the men are w^i^lling to risk loosing their horses on their way from Texas which ~~was~~ they were willing to do without a dissenting voice and the men are to start in a few days. three or four at fatherest. Tea..= I have but little to write about as there has but little tra^n^spired since I wrote my last. I wrote to Cy yesterder ~~evening~~ Morning he is near Chattanooga Tenn..Gen= Morgan has returned from ~~K~~ Ky.. after having ca captured 1500 prisoners destroying several million dollars worth of government property besides getting several thousand dollars in specie he also recruited 800 or 900 while he was there. Gen.. Forrest also did a great deal of damage to the Feds.. in Tenn.. and Ky.. he performed one of the greatest feats yet.. he rode 62 miles burnt three bridges had two skirmishes and one tolerably hard battle. all in one day.[1]

Gen.. Morgan had about 20 men killed and wounded Cy was with Morgan. It is reported here and it is reliable too that the Fed.. army in Eeast Tenn.. were captured a few days since it is about 12,000 or 15000 strong.

The news is not confirmed yet but if it is true it will be in a few days: it is very prob~~b~~able from the fact that they have been in a criticle place for some time and their rations have been very short for some time owing to their Rail road communication being cut off by Morgan and Forest taring up about 40 miles of the Rail roads in their rear and burning all the Rail road and other briges.

I will have to close this directly for I have got nothing to write about.

Tea I had like to forgot to tell you that I wanted you and Mother to fix and send me my overcoat and a couple of shirts some socks and overshirts for us both if you can conveniently.

I have the same old compla^i^nt to make about getting letters and about the friends not writing to me.. The 8th of Aprile was the last letter I received from home though I received one from John he was then near

Paris in Lamar Co.. he was well.. it was written on the 13th of July. John Grist is dead he died at a hospital in the Southern part of this State. I will now close. Give my love to all the girls and all other enquiring friends. I remain your brother Sam=

1. Presumably the First Battle of Murfreesboro fought on July 13, 1862.

Letter 41

Tupelo Mss.. Aug.. the 11th 1862
{{Near the Mobile and
Ohio Central R..R..

Dear Father and Mother

I have generally Wrote to Tea because it is more conveniet for her to answer than it is for you but I thought I would write to you a few lines this time as well as her.

We are all well at present except Joe and there is nothing the matter but diarrhea. But the main thing that I am to write about now is my horse.

Gen.. Price has given Col.. Ross permission to mount this Regt.. if the men ~~are~~ were willing to risk loosing their horses which was readily agreed to and I want Father to Send me ~~a horse~~ and John a horse and I want you to try to get me a larger horse than the Black and John one that is larger too for I found that notwithstanding the Black was as good as ever was of his size he was not strong enough but I donot want you to make too much sacrifice to get another one for us. If you cannot get a better horse than the Black do not send him for he has had the Sweny[1] and a hard ride would bring it back on him.

Father I want you and all that have friends or relations in this Regiment to aid the man that comes after the horses for this company as much as it is in your power to do for you have no idea of the anxiety of the men of this Reg^{t}.. to get them for we have been run to killing almost ever Since we have been Infantry.

Those living in peace and quiet at home can have som idea what it is to march 18 and 20 miles a day over bad roads and carry a cartridge box full of ammunition a heavy blanket 3.. 4 or 5 days rations and a heavy gun.

The fact is just reduced to this that before I or any one else in [the] Regt.. would go as infantry 2 years longer we would sacrifice every thing we have got of this worlds goods.. but this is not all: Gen^{s} Price Maury and Phifer and even VanDorn think this Reg^{t}.. can do better service ~~than~~ as cavalry than Infantry the cavalry that we have got here now is not worth much the reason I think is this..they are not good riders and they hav.nt the confidence in themselves and I have ~~hea~~ even heard some of them say that it was perfect folly to have them as cavalry and us Infantry I knew nothing about Infantry service before I tryed it. It is killing on men. If Jefferson Mabrys Saddle is at your house do you if you pleas send it to him.. it is the Saddle that John rode home on if John does..nt take it for he bargained for it before he left. I also want you to have mine and Johns Saddles rigged with some plain strong rigging for it will be impossible for us to have them rigged here and if you can get a couple of bridles and a couple pr.. spurs. And if it is possible for you to get a pr.. of boots made by Brooks at Corsicana I wish you would do it if the chances to send them are good for as pr of winter boots would cost $25 dollars[2] here and I will need a pair if you get them tell to be shure to make them high in the instep and ful sised 8^{s}. John Aycock wants you {{ if Co^{l}.. Perry do..not get his letter}} to tell him to send him a saddle.

I send you $40 so that it may assist you some in doing what I have requested you to do.

I have nothing more to write. Give my love to all the relations and all enquiring friend.

With these few lines I remain
with filial regard yours Son Sam=

1. Sweeny is a rare but debilitating shoulder injury in horses.
2. In 2015, the boots would cost over five hundred dollars.

Letter 42

Nathan Bedford Forrest's capture of Murfreesboro on July 13, which diverted Union forces from a drive on Chattanooga, was one result of continuous Confederate raids into Tennessee by Forrest and Colonel John Hunt Morgan. In the letter that follows, Cyrus describes Morgan's August 12 capture of Gallatin, Tennessee.

At Camp about twenty miles S. E. of Kingston ^Tenn^
August 18th A.D. 1862
Jas M & T A Loves:

Dear parents:

I sent a letter by hand to you a few days ago but as it may not reach you I write again by the hands of another man returning To Texas from the regmt. This leaves me in the enjoyment of good health and also the other boys from Limestone Co: except Walter Wood Bulger Peoples and William Brooks— the latter will get a discharg this evening the other two will possibly get discharges after we return from the expedition into Middle Tenn which will start tomorrow morning at 4 O,c the expedition may extend as far up as Ky and may be out for sometime and possibly will not return to this place atall as we are likely the advance guard of Genl Braggs army which from appearances are now about to make a general move into Tenn toward Ky— We learned yesturday that Morgan had passed out by cumberland gap toward Ky and had attacked and captured or killed some six or Seven Hundred of the enemy at Gallatin Tenn and also that a courier from Buel had been captured with a message from Buel demanding conveyance for his troops amunition and baggage so that he may be able to fall back toward the Northern States or rather as we would say retreat from the dangers of being whipped and captured by our forces= from what we learned yesturday the enemy have retreated from Cumberland Gap and there is now no doubt that our Commanders intend making a general move against the enemy from all parts of East Tenn—There is hardly any doubt but there are Seventy five to One Hundred thousand of our troops from Chattanooga to Knoxville=The enemy will no doubt soon be driven from Tenn and I think from Kentucky also

My horse is worn down so he cannot travel and I do not know now whether I will go with this expedition into Middle Tenn or not Some of the boys who have good horses may not go if they do not I may get a horse from one of them.

I can write but little as we are preparing two days rations for ourselves and horses. Hoping the almighty will protect us and bring us together again I remain fillially your^{s}

CW Love

Letter 43

Rangers Camp Rhea Co Tenn
August 20th 1862
Ja^{s} M & T.A. Love^{s}:

Dear parents:

It has been some time since I wrote to you or any other person in Texas and I have not received a letter from any one since I left Ft. Donaldson until yesturday evening when I rec^{d} one from Saml in which I learn that John W had been at home and left there on the 14th of June or July—he states that you were all well at the time John left you and that he was well at the time of writing (the 8th of this month) and that he wished to ascertain whether he and John could join the reg^{mt} to which I belonged—he said they wished to join cavalry on account of Johns Knee—he supposed from what he says in his letter that I was with Morgan the last time he went into Kentucky—I was not with Morgan but was with Forrest up through Middle Tennessee was in the fight at Murfresboro— and at the burning of the bridges near Nashville of which you have had an acct before this no doubt. we killed and captured about 1500 men at Murfresboro and about 100 at the bridges among those taken at Murfresboro were Genl Crittenden and Diffield a Col Parkhurst and their provost Marshal named Rounes. also also the Staff officers of both the $Genl^{s}$ and a good many captains and Lieutenants. There was but one Lieut and he the only commissiond officer taken at the bridges—We also made a trip to Manchester from McMinnville and took about twenty of their pickets one of them a Lieut but finding the enemy were too strong for us to attack them in the town we fell back about two miles formed line of battle and waited an hour or two for them to come out on us which if they had done would in my opinion have been the cause of their getting an other pretty severe drubbing they got reinforcements or rather another force from toward Nashville of about 40,000 or 50,000 came down on us and chased our pickets from McMinnville out some three miles to where our camp had been some days before we were however camped at the time about eleven miles from there on the road toward Sparta where we went in a day or two after the enemy followed after us in that direction and about one Hundred and fifty of their cavalry who were in the advance were attacked by about the same number of our men who had a small Mountain Howitzer[1] which they fired three or four times and the enemy took to their heels with all speed to get back to their infantry— I have heard that a courier went back to the infantry at such speed as to nearly kill his horse— the news he took back was that if the cavalry that were fighting us did not get help very quick they would be cut all to pieces— We knew they were too strong for us to give them much of a fight and had also been ordered to cross the Mountains[2] the third time which we did the next day after this little Skirmish— the many came on up to Sparta a day or two afterward— One of the Lieuts of this Reg^{mt} was at a house on the side of the road as they came up—a regular lubberly Paddy[3] asked him for water which he gave him— Paddy then asked him how long since the Southern boys left there and said they had been after us six weeks but could not catch us—The impious contemptible and lying sheet at Nashville[4] published that one company of their cavalry chased all of Forests forces from the bridges and run ^them^ clear away but instead of being run off we camped in six or seven miles of the bridges that night and the enemy at Nashville were very frightened so much so I understand that some of them stacked arms to surrender

Morgan, Forrest and Starnes have gone toward Kentucky, at this time I expect they are high up in Ky— Morgan started first and went over the Mountain some where about Big Creek Gap— after passing the Mountain as far as Cumberland River he sent back for Forest to come to his aid—I have not as yet been able to learn what for as we have had two reports about it—the first was that a large force of the enemy were in his rear and a regiment of them on the opposite side of the river so as to prevent him from crossing—the purport of the report was that he was surrounded The next report was that some point on the Cumberland he had a pretty large force of the enemy hemed in and wanted Forrest to help him take them if either report is true it is more likely to be the latter than the former as it would be almost impossible to hem Cavalry with infantry especially where the officers are vigilant as Morgan—My opinion from all that I can learn is that Morgan, Forrest, Scott and Starnes with a reg^{mt} or two of Tennessee Cavalry are going into Kentucky to destroy army Stores and railroad bridges—The result of Morgans previous trip into Kentucky and Forests operations at Murfresboro was that Buels forces at Steveson[5] and the mouth of Battle Creek were on half rations for eight days. but they supplied themselves by cutting the peoples green corn—Buel has become afraid that he will be surrounded as he has indicated to his Government by a dispatch that was captured by some of our troops in which he asks for transportation to fall back out of Tenn I hope the present movements of our army will cause him to be under the necessity of falling a good deal farther back than the limits of Tennessee or if he does not that he and his whole force may be captured very soon.

Genl McCook was killed a short time back by some partizan Soldiers the enemy in revenge hung seventeen citizens they charge the killing McCook as an assassination but the facts are that they wish to excuse their brutality toward the citizens. McCook with his body guard were some two miles in advance of the main force where a body of our partisan warriors made a charge on them and in the fight they killed McCook as other men are killed in an open fight and and not as the enemy report by being shot from behind the bushes. I think from from all I can learn from the Northern States that it will be almost impossible for Lincoln to get the last troops he has called for he has called out three hundred Thousand in one call and in anticipation of difficulties with Europe has called out as many more but the people seem to be opposed to it and will come unless drafted and many strong Abolitionists are running of to Canada to avoid the draft—I saw an account of forty going from one little town in Maine—it is also reported three of the States refused to give their quota of the first three hundred thousand—Pennsylvania connecticut and Ohio—it is also stated that Vellandingham[6] is stumping the state of Ohio against the war policy of the Government

In anticipation of being drafted thousands of men in the northern states are holding themselves in readiness to hire Substitutes and some of the substitutes are pocketing the money and running off with it= the price of a Substitute is said to be about $1000.00 generally[7]—their troops in Tennessee are deserting at the rate of from three to five a day so that their army will not be increased much by their recruits— the East Tennessee renegades are tired of the war also and a great of them want to get away and come home and it appear that some Regiments of them about Cumberland Gap are guarded to keep them from running off.

I understand that Buel has some five hundred at work fortifying Huntsville and about four hundred fortifying Steveson but if Braggs forces get in behind him as ^I^ think they will very soon these fortifications will do him no good—.

I will return to my old Reg^{mt}. as soon as the Rangers get back again. It is necessary for me to have a pass from this Regmt so as to get a passport on the Rail R. and by any other means necessary to get to Jackson Miss where I understand our Reg^{mt} is to be reorganized. I understand that all the ft. D. prisoners are to have furlows for a number of days if so I may come home if not you will direct your letters to greggs Regmt in the same manner as you did befor— but I will write again as soon as the Regmt is reorganized and let you know where to direct.

I have never learned how many of the Reg^{mt} had got home but have heard that a good many went home immediately after the capture of the Regmt—after the Regmt is reorganized I understand the brigade to which it belongs will be brought together at Chattanooga—All I can say now is that I hope the war will end so that I may come home this winter

Hoping the blessings of Deity will continue with all of us I will close.

Yours in fillial regard
C.W. Love

[?][8]

1. A portable twelve-pound cannon.

2. Cumberland Mountains.

3. A pejorative slang term for an Irishman perceived as lazy or stupid.

4. Possibly the *Daily Nashville Patriot*, a Unionist publication. According to the Library of Congress, the Patriot ceased publication by April 1862, but it may have continued publishing under a different name.

5. Stevenson, Alabama.

6. Clement Vallandigham (1820-1871) of Ohio was a member of the US House of Representatives from 1858-1863. A southern sympathizer, he led a group of antiwar Democrats known as Copperheads.

7. Such substitutions were written into Federal law with the Enrollment Act of March 3, 1863, which allowed two options for men wishing to avoid the draft: a commutation fee of three hundred dollars or a substitution fee, which could reach up to a thousand dollars.

8. Below Cyrus's closing, there is another, illegible signature.

Letter 44

This is a rare instance wherein the envelope is a part of the letter; it was sealed with red wax, some of which is still present. The envelope is postmarked "Sept the 8th Chapel Hill."

Tupelo Miss..Aug..the 25th 1862

Miss Tea Love,

Dear Sister

Johnnie Plesants has been discharged and I thought I would write you a few lines to let you know that we are all well yet and in fine Spirits because we are in hope of getting our horses soon.

There is but little prospect of us leaving this place very soon for they have sent all our wagons off to the Southern part of the state for the purpose of pasturing the mules.

It is reported that ,30000, Fed.. troops have landed at the junction of the Yazzoo ~~and Mss. Rivers~~ with ^the^ Mss.. River ~~and if it is~~ twelve miles above Vicksburg for the purpose of taking that place and if it is true= the next move we make from here w will be in that direction. It is also reported that Gen.. Bragg is moving from Chattanooga in the direction of Nashvill though it is not confirmed yet.= Gen.. Morgan has gone back in to Tenn.. and took Gallatin (a large town in the state) burnt 40 cars took several hundred improved Springfield rifles also great quantties of Ammunition and medical stores. I have not heard the particulars yet= it is repor= that they took all without a fight though they had..nt been gone more than four hours before 1200 Feds.. entered the town but they were too late. Cy is with Gen.. M.. I guess. I know if no other news to write.

Tea I want you and mother to make and send me several shirts 3 or 4 pr socks one or two pr drawers &.. C.. and I want you to teel others to do the same for it is going to be impossible for us to get souch things here but worse than all do I want Father to send me a pr.. of Boots for it is impossible for us to get them even now. Capt.. Ross got back from Mobile day before =yesterday. He ~~b~~ bought a pr.. shoes (just such as I have bought for $5. and $6) and had to give $18..^1/000^ for them so that a good pr.. of Boots at the same ratio would cost $35 or $40, and the most common brogans are selling from $8 to $10 the reason of the high prices is the scarsity of leather and the great demand there are thousands in the army that are barfooted and cannot get shoes and the reason that I write to you is because the demand is not so great at home and I will need a pr..of Boots this winter if I should not get a furlough for it is likely that we will have a good deal of scouting to do if we should be so fortunate as to get our horses which is very probble. When speaking of myself I have not included John but he will need as much as me. I hope the citizens will do what they can to get clothing for their friends and relations in the army. The people ^here^ are willing to do all they can but they have got so many in the field that they cannot do much for the Texians. So we will have to depend upon the citizens of Texas. If they should start with clothing I would say this that the bes and safest rout would be to come to Sims Port on Bayou Atchafalaya and there they will be likely to find steamboats they could put a wagon on there and land it on this bank of the Mss River with less danger than any other I think and then bring it out to the Rail Road and ship it to us directly. It is getting late and I will have to close.

This leaves us all well and God grant that it may find you all enjoying the same blessing.

Give my love to all the family and to all enquiring friends and to yourself the same. Tell all the Friend and relations to write to me. I am in haste you brother..Sam..

N..B.. Tell Ellen Fannie and Bettie that they might write to me once and a awhile.

Tea I must tell you one thing that is a little strange it is this there are a great many pretty girls in this country and not one of the boys seem to pay the least attention to them not withstanding there are some great ladies men here men that you would think would pay attention to them on every possible occasion but it is not the case they seem to have become perfectly indifferent to the charms of beauty but I think it is not likely they will continue so long after they get back home

All the Donaldson prisoners have been exchanged[1] for and we have been looking for Gregg[s] Regt [here] for several day [?][2]Sam..

1. On July 22, 1862, a formal prisoner exchange was agreed upon by both North and South. This agreement eventually broke down as the Confederacy refused to consider black Union soldiers prisoners of war.

2. A tear in the page obscures the word here.

Letter 45

This letter is written directly after Second Manassas (also known as Bull Run) in Virginia, from August 28-30, 1862, which opened the Potomac to Confederate advance. Though Sam gets the facts in this letter generally correct, he is optimistic with his predictions. For example, General Lee did advance across the Potomac, but did not gain possession of Washington City. Nelson was mortally wounded at a later date by his own man, not during this battle. There were only five thousand men captured, not nine thousand as Sam suggests.

This letter resembles a journal entry for Sam, as it covers the span of two days, with a second entry added before the letter was sent to Tea. Although Sam says that he is in good health, company muster cards indicate that he was sick sometime during the months of July and August. Under General Earl Van Dorn, Sam and John are still engaged with Grant's forces in northern Mississippi, as the postscript indicates. Cyrus is still under the command of General Bragg who, along with General Kirby Smith, is pushing north into Kentucky.

Saltillo Sept the 8th.. /62

Dear Sister

Mr..Sharp and Loyd will leave this place for Texas tomorrow morning and I am attempting to write you a few lines though I have but little to write that you will not have heard before this gets to you. ~~though~~ There has been a great deal of fighting since I wrote before.

Gen.. Lee has defeated Gens.. Pope and McLellan on the plains of Manassas again and has drove them across the Potomac and very likely has possession of Washingto City or else he is bombarding it at the present moment. The Federal army in Va.. has been hopelessly defeated. Gen.. E.. K.. Smith has taken Gen Nelson and 9,000 Feds in Tenn=he parolled them all on the battle field= Gen. Nelson was mortaly wounded=Gen.. Morgan (Fed..) is besieged in the Cumberland Gap and all of his commissary stores have been cut off he will be compelled to surrender= Gen Br^a^gg is in hot persuit of Buell and trying to cut him off from Nashville= if he succeeds Buell will have to surrender if not he <u>may</u> get away. Gens.. Forrest Morgan and Armstrong are doing good service in Tenn and Ky Ky.. they have destroyed a great many Rail Road bridges tore up a great deal of the R..R.. iron Burnt the commissary stores of the army of Tenn.. taken a great many prisoners besides they have recruited several thousand The whole sum of it is this the Feds have got into an unpleasant fix

You will see ~~that~~ by the heading of this letter that we have move our camp we are about ten miles up the R..R.. from Tupelo. We moved day before= yesterday. We are steadily advancing towards Tenn but we ~~can~~ are necessarily slow because we have to build R..R.. bridges as we go for the purpos of bringing up our commissary stores. There is several thousand Feds.. at Corinth and the first thing they know we will have them in a fix. There is nothing more of importance to write so I will close this part of my letter. I have not heard anything from Cy.. for a long time I do not know the reason for I have written to him twice since I come here neither have I heard from John since the 13th of July or from any of the family since the 8th of Aprile so you may judge of my anxiety to hear from some of you I have not heard from either unkle John or unkle Andrew for a long time Gen.. Armstrong drove the feds from Denmark 4 or 5 days ago. I expect they have injured unkle John as they have done every body else. This leavs us all in good healthand hoping that it will find you all enjoying the same blessing. Give my love to all the family and relations and all enquiring friends and ~~th~~ tell them to write to me as often as they can. With these few badly written lines I remain your brother Sam..

Sept the 9th ../62

P..S. Since writing my letter I have learned that the Feds have left Corinth and our advance has taken possession of it. I cannot give an opinion about wher we will go to some say to Memphis while others say we are going to the Ohio River. It is reported here that Gen.. Brgg says that he is a candidate for military Govenor of the state of Ohio though I doubt the report. There is not the least reason now why the foreign powers should not acknolledge our Independence now they will either have to do it or acknolledge the real reason that they have not done it before. The reason in the opinion of here is that they wanted us to fight as long as possible or until we had weakened each other so much that they could come in and bag the whole of both parties so ~~that~~ they will now have to ~~hear~~ acknolledge one of two things our Independence or the reason they do not.

I was very sorry to hear of Ewing Caruthers.^{es} deth I was also sorry to hear of Mr. Archibalds being killed by his son and a little surprised to hear of McGrews death.

You may be a little surprised about how I learned this so I will tell you. Ben.. Kenady got a letter from Mrs Wash Kenady about 10 days since. It is getting late and I will have to cose this post script. From your brother

Sam.. B.. Love

Letter 46

In Camp near Baldwin Mss..
{{Sept..the 25th.. 1862

Dear Sister

I have another opportunity of writing to you again and sending it by a young gentleman that has been discharged from Capt..{{now Lt..Col.. of sharp shooters} Bridges old Co.. he goes to Tyler in Smith Co.. Tea we left Saltillo on the 11th.. of this month and marched to Iuka which place we reached 3 days after the enemy having fled before we got there but they reinforced in 2 or 3 days and come back to attack us with 30,000 or 40,000 which we had only 15,000 so we in turn had to retreat on double quick but not until they had shelled us a good deal. Our ~~brigade~~ ^division^ was sent in the advance so that we got the benefit of their shells though they done no mischief although they come very close to us. The

1st division under command of Gen.. Little was held in reserve at the town but it se^e^ms that they were destined to be the only ones ~~that~~ ~~got~~ ^to get^ into the fight for {{on Friday evening before we left on Saturday}} the Feds.. made a demonstration in our front while they sent a division around our left flank for the purpose of burning our train and attacking us in the rear and owing to the ineficiency of our cavalry come very near getting the train for the battle commenced in less than ¼ of a mile of it. The attack was brought on by gen..Herbert^{s} brigade and two Regt^{s} from Gen.. Mitchel^{s} Brig consisting in all of 6 Regt^{s} though the brunt of the battle fell on the 3^{d} Texas and 3^{d} La.. {{Greers & Herbert^{s} old Regt^{s}}} in fact they done all that effected any thing for they alone took two batteries one of 6 and the other of 3 guns they took them too from a Brigade of the best of the northorn troops they also were in a cross fire from the two batteries besides the small arms of twice their number of infantry and you may judge of how the Fed^{s}.. fought from the last fact that ^an^ Iowa reg^{t} was all either killed or wounded and the Co.. that were working the battery of 6 guns fa^u^ght until they were all except one Lt.. killed and he was wounded. There was a singular instance of bravery happened just after the battery was taken it runs thus.. Our boys had a couple of Infantry prisoners and an other come up to them and said less go.. the d=n=d= Rascals will kill us all when one of his comrades said.. We are in the hands of the sesesh. 3^{d} one says show them to me.. it was done and he made a rush at the man {{one of Greers}} with his bayonet the Confed.. caught the bayonet in his left hand and shot him with his right. The Feds say that the battery that was taken had been charged 9 times before and never taken until the 10th. Tea.. it was a short battle but the hardest of the war.[1] the two above named Regts lost killed and wounded about 400 men. Tea I have had to write in great haste and I will now have to close. We are in good health and Spirits and hope these few hastily written lines may find you and all the friends enjoying the same Gods blessing.[2]

1. Confederate casualties from the Battle of Iuka totaled 1,516.

2. The line "the same Gods blessing" is written vertically along a center fold. While this letter is unsigned, given the date, location, and style, it is likely written by Sam.

Letter 47

After the Battle of Iuka, Major General Sterling Price's troops marched to Ripley, Mississippi, where they joined forces with Van Dorn's Army of West Tennessee in what turned out to be a two-day battle, October 3 and 4, for the Union-held town of Corinth, whose inner line of defenses included a line of five batteries (forts) armed with siege guns able to lay sweeping fire on attacking forces. Although they suffered severe losses, the Confederate forces managed to storm Battery Powell and approach Battery Robinett, the scene of desperate hand-to-hand fighting.

In Camp near Holly Springs Mss..
{{Oct the 14th 1862

Dear Father & Mother

It is with the most sincere thanks to god for preserving my life in the terrible battle that we have just pas^ed^ throug that I attempt to write you a few lines to let you all know the fate of your relations and friends. In the first place.. after we had rested two or three days at Saltillo on our retreat from Iuka we started by the way of Riply for the purpose of forming a junction w with Lovell an VanDorn to attack Corinth in the rear.

After marching six days the battle opened on Friday the 3d about 5 miles from town and about 9.. O. clock our forces drove them before them very rapidly yntil we come to their first brest works about one mile in front of their second and main intrenchments when they were taken about 3.. O..Clock at the point of the bayonet and several pieces of artilery was taken from the enemy. All this had been done without our brigade being ordered into the fight though we supported severall attacking Brigades but about 4..O..Clock we were ordered to charge a battery or rather two batteries that were about ¼ of a ~~b~~ mile in front of their main intrenchments.

We ~~we~~ were about ½ a mile from it when the charge commenced. We started at a double quick and directly after we started botho of the batteries commenced throwing grape and canister shot by the bu[1]..but it did not stop us untill we had driven all the gunners and Infantry from bothe of the batteries but we could not hold it or bring it off the reason we could not hold it was we were not strong enough to fight the supports that was brought against us for we had no support atall the reason we ^did^ not bring them off Spike[2] them or brake them down was all the horses were killed we had no spikes to spike them nor axes to brake them down. But we did not do all this without a sacrifice of life as well as wounded. Of the latter was J.. B Prendergast. He was wounded ~~by~~ by a piece of shell when we were in about 100 yds of the battery that done it he fell charging as fast as he could run fortunat^e^ly though it was not a dangerous wound. The piece struck his thigh about 4. or. 6 inches below the fork the piece passing on the inside of the bone making an uggly flesh wound though it did not injure the bone. The wound is not a dangerous one attall. There was nothing else done that evening except a disposition of the forces for the attack on the 4th. There was nothing of importance done the next morning except some heavy firing of artilery which done no mischief until 10, O..Clock when the order for the attack along the whole line was given. Now comes the hard fighting. The enemy had brest works with port holes for the Infantry and artilery and ditches in the rear of them making all within very secure and besides that they had an abatis[3] of fallen timber in their front about 300 yds in width. The artilery commenced throwing grape & canister shot as soon as we come in sight and when we got into the edge of the fallen timber the Inf.. commenced firing but we still advanced on them and commenced fireing about 150 yds—We kept it up and still advanced until we drove them from their works took their artillery and planted our banners on their bre^a^st works but you can imagin our mortification when we saw a coloum advancing to the support of the Fed^{s}. about twelve deep then we turned to see if we had any support and there was none to be seen the result was we had to give up all that we had taken at a sacrifice of the life of some of our best boys besides a great many wounded. There was 23 killed wounded and missing in our Co.. and 145 in our Regt and about 550 in the Brigade. There was 7 killed 4 missing and 12 wounded among the wounded is Capt Ross and Lt.. Wilson. Pete Lewis is counted among the missing though he was not in the fight=he was taken very sick the night before we left Pocahontas 18 miles from Corinth=and left in a house near the Hatchie River and the only consolation that I can offer to his people is that he may have got well ~~got well~~..but he is certainly a prisoner for on Sunday the 5th the Fed^{s} cut off our retreat by the way we come and occupied the ground where we left Pete while we were fighting them The Fed^{s} forced us back across the river by out=flanking us= We then formed on the brow of ~~the~~ ^a^ hill about 300 yds from the river=The Feds then crossed the river to persue us but by the time they come in sight we had two batteries planted and our Brigde formed to receiv them.. Tey come up an we drove them back and they come again only to meet the same iron and leaden hale.[4]

1. Bushel.

2. Preventing ignition in a cannon by driving a steel spike into its touch-hole.

3. An obstacle formed by felled trees that have been sharpened and pointed toward the enemy.

4. At least one missing page likely follows this point. The letter is unsigned, but its style, identified by the trademark punctuation, and the fact that the next letter from Sam also originates in Holly Springs, indicates that the author is Sam.

Letter 48

Generally considered a Confederate defeat, the second Battle of Corinth discussed in Letters 47 and 48 resulted in estimated casualties of nearly 2,360 on the Union side, and well over 4,800 on the Confederate. Union general William Rosecrans, the victor at Corinth, had a reputation for being rather brusque and quarrelsome—especially with his superior General Grant—but Sam notes that he treated captured Confederate soldiers well.

In camp near Holly Springs Oct. th 20. /62

Dear Sister

I embrace the present opportunity of writing you a few lines to let you know how we are getting on also to tell you a few more of the particulars of the battle of Corinth and the first and best part of it is.. one of the boys of our Co.. that we all thought was kille come in this morning and brings the report that two others that we were shure were kill.. one of them was badly wounded and the other not hurt. the one that come in is by the name of Cobb the othe two.. Collier and Sharp Collier was not hurt but John Sharp was wounded in the head twice and is now at Iuka 30 miles from Corinth on the Memphis and Charlston R.. R.. one of the balls ~~went in at~~ touched his nose ^slightly^ and the other in the back part of his head making ~~a couple o~~f^one^ wounds that ~~are~~ ^is^ very bad but a young Dr = {Talley} of our Co.. who was wounded slightly and taken to the same place § but has returned on paroll[1] with Cobb § says that he do..nt think it will prove fatal. Talley also says that J.. B.. P.. Ben Kenady and the others of our wounded that were left ~~on~~ ^in^ the hands of the feds are doing very well and that the piece of shell that wounded Joe went through thereby saving him a great deal of pain for it would have had to be cut ~~off~~ out. Tehy are well cred for and well treated.

Gen. Rozencratz ^Fed..rl^ says that men that fight like Maury[s] shall be well treated. And one I like to have forgotten is Pete Lewis. The other night greatly to the surprise of us all he stepped into camps but very sick from the chollick[2] though it was not long till we had him relieved and next morning he was well and has been well ever since. About the battle I ^have^ but little more to say.. only I can give you the order of attack an near the number of killed wounded and missing of the whole army. The attack on friday was as follows. the 1st Division of Prices Corpse was in the advance and drove the enemy before them untill they come to the first intrenchments where Gen.. Moors Brgade was thrown forward to assist in taking them and it was done directly after which fireing ceased for 15 or 20 minutes and then commenced a battle of artilery along the whole line which lasted about half an hour.. it was terrific.. there was about 100 pieces of artilery of the largest field calliber fireing as fast as they could. After half an hour Gen.. Moors Brigade was attacked by a superior force and the Reg[t]. of Sharp Shooters that belong to our Brigade and our Reg[t] were ordered to the right to assist them and the Feds saw us coming and fell back to their intrenchments.. in the mene time the other two Reg[ts] of our Brigad were ordered to the front to attack a party that had come out from their ints[3].. and we were then ordered to the left to help them= we charged two batteries but as I said in my other letter we had to give them up.

This was about all that was done on Friday the 3[d]..

On Saturday morning our troops were disposed along the whole line for the purpose of a making a general attack they were in this order.. The first Division under Gen.. Herbert was on the right and center his left forming part of the center and the second Division under command of Gen.. Maury on the left the right of the division forming part of the center while Gen.. Lovell[s] Devision was held in reserve not one of the attacking columns had any sup^p^ort The result is stated in my other letter but for fear that you should..nt get that I will say here that every Brigade done its duty for we took the intrenchments and held them until overwhelming numbers were brought against us. And there we were in an enemys intrenchments with 3 or 4 to one against us and no Support. It was a badly managed affair on the part of our Commanding Gen. Van Dorn. We~~nt~~ ^sent^ back a party to bury the de^ad^ but the Feds wouldnt let them go to the battle ground they said they were burying them and that they were burying them decently for said they men like them deserve it. When they come to our boys the first thing they said was well boys have you got sober.. They say we were all drunk for they say no Sober man would undertake to do what we done and the boys could not make them believe anything else. After ^the^ battle on Saturday we camped about eight miles from Corinth= the next morning early we commenced the retreat again and after marching about five miles we learned that the enemy from Bolliver had possession of the bridge over the hathie river[4] so they put us out at quick [time][5] 5 miles and double quick[6] a mile= Our [Brigade][7] and Moors crossed the bridge but we had to give up the position we had for they were flanking us on both flanks we fell back to a hill on ¼ of a mile from the river and formed along the crest of a hill where our battery came to us and took position 2 guns on the right and 2 on the left=We were not there long before we saw the Feds marching by the right flank in about 150 yards of us some said they were friends and some said they were Fed[s] but we were not long in being undeceived for as soon as they come to the river they formed and here come a volley of smal arms but they did..nt stay there long for we all turned loose on them battery and any and they run like Scared Sheep but they formed and come again though [it][8] was only ~~th~~ to met the same leaden hale [then] they run again—by this time however they had crossed enough troops to outflank us so we had to fall back again all this time there was no Brigade but ours engaged in the fight. In [a like] ~~m~~ manner we fell back [till] we come to Rusts.. Brigade which was perfectly fresh..

when they took command of the rear and we went along with the train.

We marched all that night and the next day until 12 O.. clock.. and the next day and night.

The loss of the army in killed is 800 the wonded is about 2,000.. the missing about 1,200 making a aggregate of 4,000 killed wounded and missing=the prisoners are all returning on parole. Tea I will have to close this part of my letter. You must not feel dispirited because of our defeat for there is not a man in the army that feels himself whipped for we feel confident of our ability to whip them if our Gens.. will give us a showing.

Gen.. Pemberton superceeds Van Dorn in the command of this army and we look to hi~~s~~m for better ~~s~~ results.

I have not heard from Cy in 3 or 4 months. Though I believe he is doing well.

The Donaldson prisoners are here though I have not se^e^n any of them=they are all ordered to report to their respective commands so I shall look for Cy soon. Tea do not too confidently ^look^ for me this winter fo I do..nt know whether I will get a Furlogh[9] or not [though][10] I am going to try for one. John is here with the [horses][11]=some of them are in tolerable order while [others][12] are thin=my pony is looking well.

I will have to close this by Sending my Love to Nannie Serena and Mollie especially and all the girls in general. ~~and if you see~~ Tell Fannie that I was glad to receive a few lines from her this time and would be glad to receiv them often. Give my love to Fannie Bettie and Ellen and all the other relations but particularly to Mother Father Robt and Tennessee and tell Robt I would be glad if he could come with some clothing but boots particularly this fall but he is too young to go into the service[13]

With these lines I remain your brother Sam.. B.. Love N. B. Tell Unkle Bakers family not to feel the least uneasiness about Joe for he is doing well Sam

1. Lacking a means for dealing with large numbers of captured troops early in the war, the US and Confederate governments relied on a system of parole and exchange of prisoners such as the one described in Letter 44. The terms called for prisoners to give their word not to take up arms against their captors until they were formally exchanged for an enemy captive of equal rank. Generally, parole was granted within a few days.

2. Colic, acute abdominal pains caused by abnormal condition of the bowel, was one of the most prevalent illnesses in Confederate camp.

3. Entrenchments.

4. Hatchie river.

5. An ink stain obscures this word.

6. Quick time standard pace is 120 beats per minute with a 30 inch step. Double quick is a moderate jog.

7. An ink stain obscures this word.

8. A vertical tear obscures the wording here.

9. Confederate soldiers were typically given sixty-day furloughs, though their issuance became severely restricted as the war progressed.

10. A tear in the page obscures part of this word.

11. A tear in the page obscures part of this word.

12. A tear in the page obscures part of this word.

13. At this time white men ages eighteen to thirty-five had been conscripted for the duration of hostilities, and Robert was fifteen years old as of Sam's writing. It was not uncommon, however, for younger men to volunteer.

Letter 49

Apparently returning from a furlough, John writes his parents and sister to assure them of his safe journey back to camp. The two letters below are enclosed together with the same date: one written to the Love parents and one to Tea. There are few letters written by John Love within the collection, so these letters are noteworthy.

This Union post office is typical of the kinds of impromptu accommodations for mail delivery necessary during the Civil War.

Camp near Holly Springs Oct 20th 62
J.M. Love Esqr

Dear father I have got to the boys I found some of them in very bad health Sam is in good health & has the appearance of ~~of~~ a good ~~health~~ ^soldier^ He has been in several fights since he come over the river The last fight he was in was a very serious one there was 14 wounded & [10] killed out of our co. Sam had a hole shot through his cap Joe Prendergast was wounded in the ~~thigh~~ thigh he was the first one wounded: Ben Kennedy was wounded in the arm John Sharp was wounded in the head.

A horse-drawn wagon delivering mail to troops in the field.

Joe & Ben are seriously wounded & John is dangerously wounded so we hear Our Captain was wounded in the chin & arm We have the bravest and best captain in the service. Our horses look very well I Swapped Morgan[1] off he was too tender he had fallen away a great deal I got a large one 8 years old I ^am^ going to sell him to the artilery for about [300] three hundred & fifty dollars & buy me a good cavalry horse for about three hundred we have heard nothing of Cyrus yet he is away up in Ky or Tenn. Pa I don't know of anything else to write about now. Sam is writing he will give you all the news— give my love to Ma & all of the family your Aff[2] son John

1. Presumably John's horse.
2. Short for affectionate.

Letter 50

Camp near Holly Springs ^Miss^ Oct 20th 62
Miss Tea Love

Dear sister I have got to Sam at last. We had no trouble in crossing the river. I come & saw [Mat] R & cousin Mollie. Sam was just about out of every thing when I to him his shoes was worn out his hat was about gone & I gave him the one you fixed for me it makes him look very well Pete Lewis has been sick a long time he was left behind & the feds got him but he beat them yankeeing & got away from them he is here in camps & looks to be improving If Pa could get us a pair of boots made & send them to us it would save us paying 45 dollars for them here a common hat— 15 a pr of shoes 15 an overshirt made ^out^ of common [liney][1] is worth $7.50 a pr. socks is worth $2.00 a hickory shirt is worth $5 & $6 apiece a drawers from $3.50 to $5.00 & every thing is in proportion Tea I have nothing else to write give my best love to Nannie and Lizzie tell Nannie that I would write her a few lines if I thought she would answer it.. Give my love to all the family & accept the love of your brother John W. L

1. Possibly linen.

Letter 51

Camp Ross[1] Nov the 28/62

Dear Sister

Maj=White is going ^to^ start Home this morning but I did not know it until it was too late to write you a long letter. I will have to make this very Short for I have to go on review in a few minutes and he is going to start at 10 o'clock. There is nothing of importance here that I no~~w~~ of the enemy it is reported are trying to flank us by marching down the Mss River though the report is not generally believed. Our bonys have been on several Scouts to within [10][2] miles of Memphis but found no Feds. It is reported that gen= Kirby Smith is on the Mobile and Ohio R..R.. with 15..000. men. It is not believed here. I See in Petes.. letter from his mother that you had heard that Gen.. Price was killed at Corinth it is not so Gen.. Price doess not put himself in so much danger as the citizens think he does though for all that he is a brave [man and a good Gen][3] but his bravery and generalship is both overrated. If the Corinth battle had been a success he would have got all the praise while as it turned out the whole blame fell on Van Dorn on who[s] h^e^ad it should fall. But what I object to is not giving prais or sensure to the proper one. I will now have to close John will write more We are all well. Give my love to the family and relations and to all my friends With this I remain your

brother Sam

Mr. J.M. Love

Dear father Sam has finished his letter to Tea & I thought I would just write a few lines on this.. I have not been well since I got here I have had the chills & fever since I got here mixed with Pneuralgia I have got to be very poor I am thriving now Pa I would send you some money but I only drew three months pay so we will need all we have got our horses are doing very well I have a better horse than I had at first & some boot.

All the boys are all well from our co. Goodbye

J W Love

1. Near Jackson, Mississippi.
2. There is a tear in the page here.
3. There is a tear in the page here.

Letter 52

By the end of 1862, the Army of Northern Virginia had pushed into Maryland while Bragg retreated back toward Tennessee. Further west, Grant began his assault on Vicksburg.

Most of the letters in this collection are in excellent condition, but this letter is an exception. The two pieces of paper (written on front and back) of the letter have significant tearing along the edges. The letter's line breaks have been replicated, and [?] used to illustrate where the page is torn and where words are missing at the beginning or end of a line.

Camp Wharton near Gren[?]
Dec.. the 11th 1862

Dear Sister

I have but little
to write to you this time though you
will hear of the battle of Oakland
in which this Brig.. was the only acting
on the part of the C.. S.. and the Kansas
Jahawkers[1] on the part of the U..S..

In the first place: we started on
a Scout from our camp on the [?]
hachie River for the purpose [?]
after a Brig.. of Fed.. Cavalry 3000 [?]
and prevent them from getting posse [?]
Panola a depot on the R..R.. but they [?]
their course toward Grenada Still far[?]
down the R..R.. and on the South Side of the [?]
busha River [2] So it happened that they [?]

start of us but we managed to get betwee[?]
and Gren.. but they got to within[?]
of it. We then turned up the country in
per^s^uit of them riding all the first day
through the rain but the Second day was
fair and clear. We marched 6 or [7 mi]
to Oakland formed a line of battle and
rested till we got some potatoes § our bread
having give out §We then marched on
{{Our co. and two others one fro[?]
and one from Whitfields Regt^{s}. [?]
the advance guard}} about 200 y [?]
loaded and then marched on[?]
[?] then marched 250 or 300 yds. when
[?] of our [vidętts] discovered the enemy
[?]ing up the hill and fired on them
Here I had better state the order of
battle Col.. Mabry^{s} Regt had been sent
to the rear of the enemy while Whitfeild
and Rosse^{s} were just behind the vanguard the van=
guard and Wht^{s} Legion
dismounted and charged them before
the 6th could get up. The Fed^{s} give
[?]round and then run like Turks
[?]they did.nt get off without a round
[?] us. We drove them away from one
[?] their batteries and took it they then
[?]ted another on us and Lt Co^{l}.. Griffith
[?]ng Brigadier}} was forming us to charge
[?] at which time the he expected the 3^{d} to
[?]rge on horseback in the rear but unfor

[?]ately Lt Co^{l} Hawkins just as we were
[?]d come galloping from the left and
told Col.. Griffith that they were flanking
us on the left with heavy columns of
infantry. Co^{l}.. G.. then ordered us to
[?] horses ~~to and~~ to retreat. We could
not bring off but one of the pieces of
artilery because part of the horses in
the other pieces were killed The
[?]at they were flanking us was
[?]ue and if we had known it we
[?]d have had one of the worst
[?]eed among the Fed^{s} that was ever seen.
[?] the fight we retreated 10 [mis]
[?] The next morning we receive
[?]~~another~~ reinforcements and went back
but they had taken a scare and left
on double quick and we after persuing
them a short distance returned to camp
to get rations.. for we had all ready been
out 8 days on 5 days rations.—
Nothing of importance has transpired
since we came to camp. We are looking
[?]ders to go on another Scout soon.
[?] reported that Gen.. Jos.. E. John=
[?] is in Grenada and that he is
[?] to take command of this army.
[?] not heard from Cy.. Since
[?] last spring I do..nt know
[?] to writ to him. I have not heard
[?] Joe.. Baake.. but I have no doubt

[?] doing well. John is not well
[though] he is improving he has not
been very sick myself and all the
rest of the boys are in excellent health
The health of the Brig.. is very good.
Give my love to the family and relations
and to yourself a portion Give my love
to Nannie Serena and Mollie
[Direct] your letters thus. S B Love
~~[?]end~~ Grenada Mississippi care
[?] of Capt Ross 6th Reg^{t} Texas
[?] cavalry 1st Texas brigade army
of East Tenn..
I have not received a [?]
from you or any one els[?]
months except the one [John brought]
I cannot tell the reason for all
the rest of the company receive
them readily enough. The only
reason I can think of is you forget
to pay the postage.[3] If it is not
payed I will not get them.
Write long letters and write [often]
and tell others of the fa[?]
write. I have nothing [?]
to write ~~by~~ but remain[?]
brother Sam..

1. Jayhawkers were a band of antislavery, pro-union guerillas located in Kansas and Missouri.

2. Yalobusha River.

3. Due to irregular Confederate postage rates, citizens often had difficulty determining how much was owed.

Letter 53

Chatfield Dec. 14th 1862

Dear Mother[1]

I have waited patiently a long while for Tea or Boby[2] to write and now I will get you to try and pursuade them to write for I am very anxious to hear from you all. the latest news from the~~y~~ boys and how you are all getting on. I do think Tea has treated me badly. I feel her negligence [?][3] very much I have not written it is true. I have been so busy—since I came home that I have had hardly time to draw a breath untill now we have to make Brother [Jessies] clothes allmost evry thread of them and you know we have not been idle. but if Tea [?][4] [would write I would have] one hour of pleasure in replying. I fully intended writing by [Jimmie] but Frank and Mollie Neal would have me to gon home with them. I told Ma to write a few lines for me and from Tea.s reply it could not have been many. Mother if I ^am^ some time neglec^t^ful my heart is as it always was. you know and understand my [feelings] better than any one else. for ^I know Mother^[5] that you are my lone simpathiser Mother from what Jim could tell me ~~that~~ you did not take our drapes for overshirts. I was glad to get the one I did: but if I had known that you was [not] going to take the drapes I should not have sent to you for one. For I know how you had to work and am afraid you could not spare it well.

did you send the boy any clothes. did ^you^ have an opportuni^ty^ of sending them ^[rather]^ I am looking for Brother every day. if he can only live to get home he has been sick since last August all most all the time. he had the chills untill a few weeks ago when he took the [Enacipalous].[6] we got a letter from him last week he said he had never in his life suffered so much his face and head was swolen so bad that he was perfectly blind for more than a week. he said this disease was broke but it had run down on his back and shoulders. he said it was so painfull that he could scarcely [?][7] ly down. he did not say any thing about comeing home in his letter. but Mrs Hank received a letter from Mr. Hank a week later in which he said Brother was getting well very fast and was comeing home as soon as he could get him a horse (he had the misfortune to loose his while he was sick) Mr. Hank says that brother is an awfull looking sight he has had his head s^h^aved. and his head and face is a solid scab.

Mother I get so impatient some days that I am nearly crazy. If Brother comes you may look for a flying visit. For I want to see you very much. Josie says evry day he is going to the dark woods to find Aunt [Tea]. Just think Mother I have to whip Josie with a switch sometimes, he is yelling so bad, but he is as smart as he is bad. he has plenty of sense. [from me] if he is my child. I know what Tea is saying. that I think Joe is smarter than common children. (so I do) I heard several days ago that Ellen was in Corsicana and that she is no better. I was supprised for I thought she was certainly getting better. Mother I have very little hope now of Ellens ever getting will. I intend writing to her next saturday and am going to see her as soon as I possable can. I want to see Ellen I have something to ask her. Brother said in his letter before the last that he saw Jim a few days before he wrote. he says his health is very delicate. he says Jim told him all about Josie. Mother Adelia Sessions is dead (Viola Haymines sister) there has been very little sickness here this fall and winter with the exception of the measels they are having them at the Bluff now we try to keep clear of them as Mollie and Josie has never had them. Josie and I have that same [sick] that Ellen had we have got it in its prime now. Ma says she has discovered some bumps on her. it scares her to think she will have it like me. Mother I do wish you would tell me what to do for it. for I know nothing about the thing only its itching and Ive learned that pretty well. you need not tell me what to do for that. Mother tell Tea or Budy one to please write to me. I feel like I was forgotten perhaps I may be I do wish I could see you to night—I think it would cheer me up. the blues has got to be an evry day thing with me. Budy promised to come up last Christmas and did not. tell him to come this. tell him to come and I will give him a cake, [plays] on it—I have to stop to [wach], I know you have. heard enough of my lingo for one time. so I will hush up. is Tennie at home I want to see her very much. give my love to all the family and except for your self the love of a Daughter

Fannie Love

P.S. you ought to see the trouble I have in trying to make Josie wear his shoes. it has been raining all day and I think if I have dried his shoes and stockins once I have a dozen times. tell Tennie Josie needs some socks very bad and sister has not time to knit them. I wonder who would.

Fannie

1. The author of this letter has not been identified, although she is certainly familiar with members of the Love family and a family member herself, either through birth or marriage. Mary Elizabeth Karner had a daughter named Frances, but records indicate that Frances Karner was not born until 1871.

2. Robert Love.

3. Two words are blacked out here.

4. A word is blacked out here.

5. These words are written above marked out text.

6. Perhaps Encephalitis, an acute inflammation of the brain.

7. A word is marked out here.

Letter 54

This letter, still attached to its envelope, tells its own story. On the upper portion are the words "C. W. Love Capt. Shannon Co. C Compliments of Texas Rangers." Captain Shannon's signature is also found on the envelope, which served as an official endorsement of the letter. According to Harry K. Charles, before mail could be sent through the Confederate postal service, soldiers had to list their rank and unit and collect the signature of their commanding officer in order to verify that the soldier was still enlisted (2012, 16). A seal with the words "Due Ten" cents is visible. The words "Compliments to Miss Polk" are also penned in Cyrus's handwriting; several math problems cover the face of the envelope. Although apparently written by Cyrus, the computations may have been added by the receiver.

Cyrus mentions General Wharton, who took command of the regiment popularly known as Terry's Texas Rangers, after the death of Benjamin Franklin Terry and Thomas Lubbock. The Rangers fought in all the major battles of the Tennessee campaign.

Camp near Triune
Franklin Co Tenn
Decr 20th /62
Ja^{s}. M. & T.A. Love^{s}

Dear parents:—I wrote an indifferent letter to you a few days ago and in it I said I would give you a history of our travels since my last letter which was from near Kingston in East Tenn.= From there we crossed the Mountains into Middle Tenn following the rear of the enemy as they went by Nashville and on up through Ky to Boling Green we then passed them and went [on][1] up to Braggs army which we passed at Glasglow and we were afterward on the left and front of the army until we were in abut twenty miles of Louisville where we turned to the East and came out at Cumberland and Big Creek Gapes down to Knoxville where we remained for some weeks when we came to Kingston where we remained a week or two and then came over to Sparta where we remained several days and from there by moderate marches we came to this place.

I will now give a few of the incidents of this long and apparently useless trip—first as the enemy began to retreat—they were in the necessity of destroying a good deal of their property and as they marched a good-many of them deserted and came to forces to be paroled we had but little fighting as we went Northward until we got Mumfordsville the place where Terry was killed (it is called Woodsonville by the Rangers) at this place. Chamers Brigade of Withers[s] Division attacked the enemy in their fortification and was repulsed—it was a foolish and wicked affair as he had only two thousand men and attacked four thousand five hundred of the enemy behind fortifications there were [about][2] two hundred of our men killed and wounded—a few days after this we surrounded the place and took it with all the wagons arms amunition and camp equippage we then went on to Boston in about thirty miles of Louisville and turned East toward Cumberland Gap as we went the cavalry picketed between our infantry and Louisville the picket put out after we got to Boston I was one of them we heard there were three thousand yankees at Lebanon junction we went there to see late at night and on the way got a citize to conduct us to the place but the Yankees had burned every thing and left we had hardly any sleep that night and next morning after going up the R.R. about a mile we stopped and the boys as quick as they were off their horses lay down on the ground and went to sleep the Yankees came suddenly on us in that fix and caused a stampede of about six ^miles^ in short order. The boys who had gone to sleep had let their horses loose and when the stampede began their horses left them consequently some twelve or fifteen of them were captured all but one of them were Geogians the Yankees persued us closely for the six miles where some twenty of us formed to fight them ten of them came up about the time we were formed—we fired and charged them wouding three of them and capturing seven—a Georgian and myself persued one of them through a cornfield to the to of a hill and saw him about one hundred and fifty yds from us and near about forty others standing in the road where we had passed a little before— there were about three hundred after abut sixty of us a part of them knowing the country better than we did cut across from the road we were on to the Boston and Bards town road expecting to cut us off four of them got down to the road at a place where Cheathams Division wagons were passing captured and stopped the train and also about—seven or eight of our boys who went back one at a time to see what was the reason for the train not coming up the first of the who went back were in the power of the Yankees before they saw them and the others came up under the impression that the Yankees were prisoners they were all however soon captured back again. When we got to Bardstown Whartons Brigade were put on the pike Road at M[t] Washington in about eighteen miles of Louisville and remained there till the Infantry had time to rest a couple of weeks and every thing then Started on the march for Cumberland Gape as we fell back our cavalry were fighting the Yankees evry day for some time clear up till we began to cross the mountains when we left M[t] Washington the Yankees were very cautious not to [press] us very fast and also not to get in our rear= they got one pretty fair lesson in this respect before we had fallen [back][3] to M[t] W by running into an ambuscad[4] we had fallen back twelve of fifteen miles and was in about five miles of Bardstown when the Yankees came to the conclusion they would surround and capture us there was enough of them to do this as they had a whole Division of infantry and several thousand cavalry to effect it with—they succeeded in getting fifteen hundred cavalry between us and Bardstown and formed in seven or eight sections across the road and their infantry and artillery were coming up on each side and in six or eight hundred yds of the road their artillery lacked about ten minutes of getting in position— we had been waiting for them to approach us on the road and Wharton being in error supposing Wheelers Brigade were guarding about Bardstown left his rear unguarded when we learned that the enemy were in our rear we started at a lope and went four miles in thirty minutes—the Cedar Snags (a Tennessee Company) and the Texas Ranger ahead when we began the fight and not more than two hundred and fifty of our men were engaged before the enemy were entirely routed and running for life— according to report about fifty of them were killed we also took forty two prisoners the next fight we [were][5] in of any consequence was at Perryville— at this there were about twenty five hundred of our men killed and wounded and the Yankees say we killed and wounded about three of them to one of ours—After crossing the M^{t} nothing of interest took place till we got here— Morgan captured over two thousand of them at Hartsville and a number of wagons some other small captures have been made but none of any consequence—we are standing picket in about ten miles of Nashville— the enemy forage near our pickets every day or two—they destroyed the machinery of a large Flouring mill at Franklin a few days ago—our scouts go in and annoy them near Nashville every now and then It is impossible to tell when a fight will take place here if it does atall—Genl Wharton has been reading the Northern papers and has come to the conclusion to bet five hundred Dollars we will have peace in two or three Months others are willing to bet we will have an armistice in one month

have not heard any thing from the boys in some time— in hopes the Almighty will spare us all to meet you again I remain as ever yours &c

C W Love[6]

1. There is a tear in the page here.
2. A hole in the page obscures part of this word.
3. There is a tear in the page here.
4. Ambush.
5. A hole in the page obscures part of this word.
6. The last line of the letter and the signature are written below the stamped side of the letter.

Letter 55

The following is a fragment in the Love family letters; based on Sam's mention of Christmas Day and the new year, we believe the letter was written early January 1863 and have placed it here.

Rear guard. They throwed some shells at us but hurt nobody. On Christmas day they were shelling us with two little pieces. After that they did not interrupt us any more. We had two men by the name of [Reiny] and Davis killed in our co.. a^n^d two wounded by the name of Ditto and Ba^s^ ye and two Burny and Peeples surrendered and one missing by the name of Renfro.

It is getting late and I have to write by a ~~fire not~~ light wood fire so I will have to close my letter soon.

We are all in good health Pete is unhurt all the limestone boys come out safe. Ben.. Kenady is here. His wound is not entirely well yet he says Joe..Bake..is doing ~~w~~ well= he is at an excellent place in Alabama Ben.. is going to try to try to get a furlough and come home= Joe.. will do the same when he gets able to come to the Regt. I have not still heard anything from Cy.. I hope there is nothing the matter with him that we cannot ~~hea~~ har of him:

I would like to hear from Jim[1] when you write.

Give my love to all the family and relations and all enquiring friends and to yourselves reserve my best affections. Give my special love to Father and mother[2]

With these ha^s^tily and badly written lines I remain your brother Sam..

N..B.. I had Like to have forgot to say a happy new=year and do.nt know if it is not a mockery to say it when a desolating war is all over our land ruining the country and killing its thousand daily and perhaps causing tears to flow from the eyes of many mothers and sisters and wives and lovers..on account of the loved ones lost in this most cruel of all wars waged by an unrelenting foe for the purpose of conquest and empire.

I will say but little on this subject..but God grant that there may be a peace soon so that both friend and foe may go home and enjoy themselves in peace and plenty. But if the Feds will have war they can have it to the bloody end for we are determined to fight them until all our means are exhausted and every man killed before we will submit to their tyrannicle rule. I will now have to close. Send this to Tea.. as soon as you get it.

A new new= yers gift to all and to all a short farewell

Sam..

1. Likely James A. Love, his other brother.

2. Since the letter mentions Tea and is signed "your brother Sam," it was probably written to Mary Elizabeth Karner.

Letter 56

In camp 20 miles north of Grenada
Jany the 12th /63

Dear Sister

I have but little of importance to write to you now for there has nothing transpired in this department since I wrote my last to interest to you.

There has been some hard fighting in Tennessee between Bragg.. & Rosencrantz Bragg got the best of the fight.

It is unnecessary for me to give any of the details of the fight as you will hear of it before this would reach you.

The Feds have retreated as far as Holly= Springs about 70 miles from [Gren].. the [cause] of their retreat was the distruction of their commissary Stores at Holly= Sprs.. Jackson and other places and the taring up of the R..R.. by Van Dorn on this side and Cheatham on the other side of the Hatchie River.

Bettie it amuse as well as interest you to have seen the Ladies of Tenn.. in marching through that portion of the country we had on our Fed.. overcoats that we captured at H..S.. and they always thought we were Fed^{s}.. until we told them better or they found out themselves for it was very hard to fool them long they would then open their Doors and come out on the streets and get as close to us as they could without getting in the way of our horses and some would Shout while others would laugh and told some would run and bring every thing they had cooked for us to eat while they would put everybody on the premises to cooking more.

I do..nt think I ever saw any people as highly elated in my life they were perfectly beside themselves with joy.. but there was one draw=back to the enjoyment of the Soldiers .. it was because we new we could not Stay there for we were not Strong enough and the thought that all those pretty girls had to be left to the <u>tender</u> mercies of the Fed^{s}.. put a damper on our enjoyment but I hope it will not be long before we can drive the hireling hosts of the north[1] to their homes and never be interrupted by them more when all can live in peace at home. I will now have to close by requesting you to send this to Father as soon as you can after you get it.

I have not hear from Cy..nor Jim.. in a long time write to me all you hear from them. We are all in good health and hope these few hastily written lines will find you all enjoying the same blessing.

Give my love to all the family and relations and all enquiring friends and reserve to your self the kindest regards of your brother Sam.. B.. Love

Tell all the friends to write to me. If they will do it I may get a letter once and while as it is I do..nt get any at all while others are getting them all the time

1. According to some estimates, up to one-third of Union troops were not American citizens, many of them mercenaries.

Letter 57

By January 1, 1863, the Union Army of the Frontier was in control of northwest Arkansas and pressing eastward, opposed by Confederate general Thomas C. Hindman, who conscripted several companies of Texas Cavalry to aid his defense of Arkansas. James Love was a part of one such company—Captain Benjamin D. McKie's Company G of the Twentieth Texas Cavalry, mustered from Navarro County in August of 1862.

In this letter, James refers to "a fight," likely the Battle of Fort Hindman, near the town of Arkansas Post, which occurred January 9-11, 1863. The battle resulted in the Confederates' surrender of Fort Hindman, which had been used effectively as a base for raids of Northern ships. The surrender of Fort Hindman opened the Arkansas River for Union control, and marked a turning point in the North's campaign for Vicksburg.

The two following letters, sent the same day, are the only extant letters from James A. Love.

Little Rock Jany 24 1863

Dear father for the first time since I have been out I seat myself for the purpose of writing to you I have written to Ellen[1] time and again but have received no answer I suppose she has not received them. I Know that if she had received them she would have answered me I have not heard from home since I left. There was a fight at the ARK fort in which we had about 3 or 4 thousand men taken we had 150 men killed and about 200 wounded The feds lost 2000 killed and as many wounded it is said that they took them to St Louis John & Tom were taken Prisoners a great many of the boys got away some of them after they were taken the feds did not take or spike any of the guns They were scared so bad by ~~and~~ McCulloch with his army I have been sick over too thirds of the time it has been raining and snowing all the time since we have been in this state ~~I w~~ I would like to have Bob[2] come and stay in my Place awhile it is impossible for a man to get a furlough unless he is a favorite of ~~of~~ the officers or he will honey them another reason for my wanting bob to come is my horse has been sick and is now so Poor that he is not fit to use if bob can come he can come to Little Rock and find out Where we are We are going to Desark[3] now to stay some time to Picket for the army We will be with Col Parsons Regt he (bob) can find us by asking at the Anthony House in Little Rock there will be some one comeing almost any time if he should come I do not want him to stay more than one or too months tell Ellen that I am trying to conduct myself as near right as Possible I have not learned to Swear nor drink [As] there is not three men in camp but what does Both give my Love to all the family and accept the same yourself tell ma that I want some milk and butter Badly let bob come if he can by the time he can get here it will be getting warmer than it is now let him ride Little Grey a horse of his make and size is better than a larger one — I must close

give my Love too all enquiring friends —nothing more from your affectionate son

Jas A Love

Direct your letters to Little Rock McKies squadron Texas Rangers

[?][4]

1. His wife.

2. His brother, Robert Love.

3. Des Arc is located approximately sixty miles east of Little Rock in Prairie County, Arkansas.

4. Signature illegible.

Letter 58

Little Rock Jany 24 1863

Dear Dick[1] I have been waiting sometime for a letter from you but have waited in vain Dick I would like to hear from you verry much We are having a rough time time of it here it has rained or snowed all the time I have not been in a fight yet nor do I want to be Dick how are you and what are you doing are you driving Joh today I— wish I was with you wee would have a good time of it When are yoo coming up here bring Bob with you and I will return with you Bring me a bottle of the old Mans wine and a ~~p~~ plug of tobacco Bring me something that is fit to eat for we do not get any thing that is fit to eat We have poor beef and bread with a little [?][2] sugar after this is said all is said oh for such times as we— have seen together Dont tell the old Lady how we are faring it may trouble her come up here dick and bring me a letter from Ellen I have never heard from her since I left home if yoo cant come write to me and tell me something about my people I am troubled about Ellen she was sick when I left [and I do not][3] know how she is This has given me a great deal of trouble Write to me soon Dick ~~I~~ I want to hear from you I must close give my love to all enquiring friends nothing more from your friend and well wisher

Jas A Love

Ellen hand this to Dick

1. Presumably a hired man or close family friend who lived at the Love residence.
2. Part of a word is marked out here.
3. A whole line is illegible here because of the smudging of the pencil.

Letter 59

Near Camp about 25 miles S.W.
from Shelbyville Tenn
Feb 18th 1863
Jas M & T A Loves:

Dear parents:

I recd your letter of Decr. 21st day before yesturday this leaves me in good health my weight is about 150lbs about one Month ago I weighed 155lbs this is several lbs more than I ever weighed in Texas—Terry Wilie has been affected very much for Several days past with a severe cold which makes his breast very sore Dick Oliver Bill Lynch and in fact all the Limestone County boys are in good health except now and then a head ache back ache or some other small affliction of such kind as these. There is hardly any thing of a general news character that you would not be likely to hear before you could through a letter from me but I will write a little about our Ft Donaldson trip. First we started from Shelbyville about the last of last Month and went by easy marches out by Franklin and Charlotte having very bad wet and snowy weather nearly the whole trip. We got to the Ft in some seven or eight days there was a good deal of snow on the ground but the skies were clear the evening we attacked the Ft It was attacked about One OClock in the evening and they fought on till near night— the enemy learned that we were coming about the time we were in seven miles of the Ft and just as we got in sight of the place two steamboats left in a great hurry and in a few hours gun Boats Mortar boats[1] and reinforcements came from above and below. Our boys drove the Yankees from their rifle pits back into the Ft and expected to renew the attack after night but this was abandoned as soon as the reinforcements came to the enemy=The Rangers were not in the fight having been sent out on the road toward Ft Henry to prevent reinforcements from coming in that direction after we had taken our position three yankee couriers coming from the Ft and going in the direction of Ft Henry were captured and one of our pickets in going to their stand met about twenty Yankee cavalry one of them fired on the Yankees killing one of their horses the whole picet then took position thinking those they had seen were only the advance of the enemy in force but they soon found out that they were only a scouting party

The result of the fight was that a good many of our men were killed and the Ft was not taken I expect a good many of the enemy were killed one piece of artilery cut down and a very fine Brass piece Globe sighted and rifled[2] was captured by the 2nd Georgia Cavalry and we brought it away with us=The undertaking from the beginning was a foolish thing Since our Brigade quit picketing above Shelbyville at a little town called Middleton about halfway between Shelbyville and Murfresboro and while we were gone to Ft. D. the Yankees made a dash on the pickets and took about 60 of their prisoners and I am very much afraid they have got cousin John Webb they took old uncle Amasa last summer and kept him in prison till he died because he would not take the oath to support their government and they threatened to hang John if they could get him and I am very much afraid they have got him this time

I have heard nothing from any of the boys later than your letter we have the report that Vandorn is coming here with about 12 000 men if this is so the boys will possibly be here in a short time.

I got a letter from Capt. W. L. Moody at the same time I got yours it seems that great numbers of the boys have died out of the old company Capt Moody is not well himself=The Almighty has protected me through all the dangers that have surrounded me during the war and I hope will still continue to protect me he has spared all your family up to this time.

I am very sorry to learn that Jo[s] Douglass is dead

From all that I can learn there is a strong probability that we will have peace in a short time I hope it may be before any more fighting takes place as I am heartily sick of such slaughter a battlefield is a horrid looking sight and I want to see no more of them of course I would not want peace except on terms honorable to ourselves but from the tone of the Northern papers I think the Northern peoples are willing to give us whatever we may ask for ourselves so we best grant them free trade free navigation of the Mississippi and make mutual agreement to maintain the Monroe doctrine[3]= the yankee armies are very tired of the war and I suppose are deserting very rapidly from Mississippi to the Potomac at least this is the report we have here=I am at the house of a Mr Mayberry some two miles from camp= I am out of money just at this time but will be payed off soon again I have not written very often but have not had much chance Hoping this will find you all well I will cease writing

Yours with filial regard &c

C W Love

Tell Ellen I saw two of her uncles near Middleton in Rutherford County I think

1. A small raft-like boat fitted with mortars.

2. A bronze cannon.

3. In his 1823 annual message to Congress, President James Monroe articulated the American foreign policy that would come to be known as the "Monroe Doctrine." In his message, Monroe issued a warning to European powers to refrain from interfering in the western hemisphere, as it fell within the sphere of influence of the United States.

Letter 60

Near Beach Grove [1]
Bedford County Ten.
March 6th / 63.
Miss E.T.G Love:

Dear Sister:

I rec^d your letter of Jany 17th about a week ago from it I learned that you were all in tolerable health except Ellen who I am sorry to learn is dead —you said nothing of how grand Pa[2] was getting along and nothing about whether father was able to use his arm any better now than when I left home= what you wrote in your letter was the first I had learned in some time about the boys but I again heard from them a few days ago they were well at that time but may be dead at this time as it is more than likely they were with Vandorn at the time he took Franklin a few days ago that is to say he whipped and captured some two or three thousand of the Federals at that place=there was a good deal of artillery firing over in that direction yesturday and day before but I have not yet learned what was the cause of it= there has been some firing of artillery over on or near the Shelbyville and Murfresboro pike today—I suppose it to be foragers shooting at each other. It is hard to tell what the Yankees are doing they appear to be concentrated about Murfresboro I think they are some what afraid to leave the way open from here to Nashville as they know we will be almost certain to destroy their wagon trains and they could not get along with=out them=None of us know when there will be another fight on a grand scale I hope it may not be atall and that we may very soon have peace=

I want you at all times when you write to me to state all you know about any and all the relatives and acquaintances any where in your knowledge= I heard day before yesturday for the first time since we started to fort Donaldson that cousin John Webb was not taken by the

Yankees at the time they captured Douglass[s] men at Middleton between Shelbyville and Murfresboro but that they took some of his stock=Vandorn is said to have taken from two to three thousand prisoners at Franklin a few days ago= from the best I can learn there is but little sickness in our army at this time

I hope this will find you in good health Tea I yet have the bible you gave me when I left home=Hoping the blessing of the Almighty may be with you all till we meet again=farewell

C W Love

Direct your letters to Shelbyville
Bedford County
Tenn

1. Beechgrove, a small community in central Tennessee.
2. Likely the paternal grandfather, Joseph Love.

Letter 61

In the spring of 1863, Grant moved toward the siege of Vicksburg and Lee continued his invasion to the North. All the Love brothers appear to be located in Tennessee at this time, with the possible exception of James. In the following two letters Cyrus refers to the Battle of Thompson's Station, Tennessee, fought on March 5, 1863, a Confederate victory.

Near Beach Grove Bedford County Tenn
March 6th/ 63.
Robt M Love:

Dear brother

I now answer your letter of Jany the 12th 1863= This leaves me in good health and if Sam and John were not hurt the other day at Franklin Williamson County they are possibly well yet I heard from them a few days ago they were well at that time I have had no opportunity to go to see them yet but when we are relieved from picket duty I will try to go and see them I hope this will find you all in good health None of you have written how Grandpa was and the last letter from Tea stated that uncle William was in bad health but none of you father Tea or yourself have said anything about how he is at the time your writing= I am very sorry indeed to learn that Jo[s] A Douglass is dead= this will be a terrible affliction to his mother but I hope will prove a cause of happiness to her in the end= None of you say any thing about uncle Bakes family or S. K. Scruggs or Betty M— or Jo Bake= all I have heard about Joe is that he was shot in the leg by a grape shot at the last battle at Corinth= I want you and any of the rest of the family who write to tell me all about all the relatives and this circumstances= Robt the great object in life is to study how to be and do good toward every living creature and no book can teach us better about these things than the bible

Yours fraternally
C. W. Love

Direct your letters to Shelbyville
Bedford County
Tenn

Letter 62

Based on its mention of the Battle of Thompson's Station, this undated letter was most likely written around March 1863.

Shelbyville
Tenn
Ja[s]. M. & T.A. Loves:

Dear parents:

I had a letter from you some time since and answered it. I also recd a letter from Terrissa and one from Rob[t] a week or so back and wrote in answer soon after receiving them but could not get Envelopes and so did not send them until this morning one of the company went to town and I sent them to be mailed= This leaves me in tolerable good health. I have a bad cold however which I attribute to having Slept in a house for two nights in succession: the other boys from Limestone are in about the same condition as myself except Dick Oliver who seems to be somewhat worse than any of the rest of us. Terry Wilie is in good health

Vandorn is here with his cavalry from Mississippi but I do not know whether Phifer[s] Brigade is with him or not and consequently can tell you nothing more about the boys than you may at the present time know= Solomon Scruggs told me that he learned they were well from a man he saw from Vandorns army but I do not believe the fellow knew whether Phifers Brigade was there or not= I have not been able to ascertain who were killed and wounded in the fight Vandorn had at Thompsons Station a short time back on the Alabama and Nashville railroad in which he lost about thirty or forty killed and somewhat more than one hundred wounded= they killed about One Hundred Yankees and wounded four or five hundred wounded and captured twenty two or thre Hundred= Thompsons Station is not far from Franklin on the road to Columbia.

We have been picketing until the last two or three days on the pike leading from Murfresboro to Winchester but we are now on the pike leading from Shelbyville to Nashville by Eaglesville and Triune: we are about ten miles in a Northe Westerly direction from Shelbyville but letters sent to Shelbyville will reach us. I have not been able to hear from from Middleton whether cousin John Webb was taken by the yankees the last time they were there or not

The yankees gave some of our pickets a considerable chase about a week ago and caught some of them= since Wharton[s] Brigade came over here they have had out two scouts one on yesturday went to Eaglesville where the yankees in pretty large force had been camped only a few hours before they followed them toward Murfresboro and captured some straglers who told our boys that it was the intention of the yankee commanders to begin an attack on Shelbyville yesturday but it was not done for if so we would have heard artillery as we are in eight or nine miles of the Shelbyville and Murfresboro pike and only ten from Shelbyville= the yankee army is no doubt concentrated at Murfresboro with the intention of making a move in some direction but none of us know which way

I have ceased to make any calculations as to when the war will end and I be permitted to come home again= I am satisfied from what I can learn of the yankee army that they are as tired of the war as we are and if peace is once made it will be a long time before either side can be induced to fight each other again= this generation at least will have to die out first= you have no doubt heard or rather read from the papers that there is a considerable degree of discontent in the northern states or rather in the united States= I cannot tell from what I have seen what it will lead to= Rosencrantz[1] has ordered that the citizens about Murfres shall not raise crops this year and to prevent it has destroyed their farming utensils about Murefresboro the fences are nearly all burned and also a good many houses= he has taken all the forage and provisions from the citizens and the richest men at Murfresboro are now under the necessity of going to the Yankee Comissaries for their daily provisions.

Do not look for me until you see and know I am at the house

Yours in fillial regard &c
C W Love

1. There is a slight tear on the page here.

Letter 63

The last paragraph of this letter is a letter fragment found within the collection and has been placed here based on its content. The undated fragment is marked below for reader reference. The letter is unsigned but is in the style of Sam Love. The added paragraph was signed by Sam.

Columbia Murray Co..Tenn ^/63^ Mch.. 16th
Miss Tea. Love

Dear Sister I receiv= your Letter of th 25th of Jany day= before—yesterday but I did not know that I would have any opportunity of sending you an answer so soon.[1]

Tea the only news here of importance is about the battle of the 5th of this month near Spring Hill it was a very hard fight the Feds had possession of a hill where they were protected from our balls while our force was exposed in an open field though we lost near the same number in killed and wounded it being between 200 and 300 on a side but we captured 2300 of them. While our brigade and Armstrongs were fighting in front Forrest went to the rear and attacked them there and they soon surrendered.

John Joe.. P.. and I were all noncombattants this time John was left back in Mss sick Joe had no gun and I was left with the train on account of my horse being sick and lame. John has not had any health since he got back with the horses and I am afraid he will have a hard spell of it. I have not heard from him since I left him on the 10th of Feb.. As soon as I hear from him I will write to you.

Tea..I was very sorry to hear of Ellens death though I was not surprised for she was very sickly. If I was half as good as Ellen I would not fear to die for I believe she was one of the best women I ever saw. John Acock Saw a great many of Parson Modrall^{s} friends at Spr.. Hill and he also saw W..F..Moor and I stayed with cousin Sallie^{s} Sister Mandy three or four days she is living five or 6 miles from Pulaskia She does..nt favor Cousin Sallie much but her manner in conversation is precisely like Sallies and I think all that is necessary for me to like her as well is to know her as I do Sallie. I also stayed with her father 2 nights and ^a^ day They were all enjoying tolerably good health.

I did.nt see Mrs Wilks though ~~that~~ ^her^ family were well. They asked me a good many questions about Sallie and I answered them the best I could. They had not heard from her in about 2 years before. The Yanks did not do them much mischief when they had possession of the country before but they ~~did not~~ are ruining the country where they go now and if they get [murry^{s}] Co.. again they will be ruined with the rest. Tell Cousin Sallie if she will send her letters to me I can send them to her people for her. If this letter gets there before Pete starts back tell her to send a letter by him and I will send it to whoever it may be directed but if it does not she might send by any one she can and if it gets to me I can send it to them

∓ Tea I forgot to tell you that we lost 8 me ^in our co..^ and one killed one of the wounded has did since a young man by the name of

Smith.

A young man by the name of Lemons was killed dead they were both from Waco[2]

[undated fragment]

We are all well or tolerably so. Pete has been sick for Two days though I believe he is getting well..There was nothing sirous the matter with him it was an attack of the Billious fever.[3] All the rest are harty and well. I am remarkably healthy at present Give my love to all the family and relations and to all enquiring friends.

Give Nannie Serena and Mollie my special regards. With these few badly written lines I remain your affectionate brothe Sam.

N..B.. Tea when you receive this you must write me a long answer Tell all the family that I would be glad to see them..but it will be a long time I fear before that can be

S..B..Love

1. According to company muster cards, Sam and John were "absent with train" during the months of January and February 1863, which may explain why Sam has not received mail until now and also why he has not written home in a while.

2. A semicircle is drawn around the last sentence.

3. Bilious fever was a diagnosis, now obsolete, used for any fever that exhibited the symptom of vomiting.

Letter 64

Shelbyville Bedford County
Tenn
March 25th 1863
Jas M. & T.A. Loves:

Dear Parents:

It has been but a little while since I wrote to you but having a good chance with a good pen and ink and tolerable paper I write again that you be the more certain of hearing from me I am not well at this time and have not been for some time past but have not felt much debilitated until within the last three or four days. I have been having Diarrhoea with loss of appetite and slight inward fever: almost the entire Regt are in a similar condition. Dick Oliver has been so for some time and is out in the country Wm Lynch & Terry Wilie are at the wagons they are however able to do duty at this time: on account of the conduct of some of the men of the various Cavalry Regts about this army we are now under tighter orders than ever before= We have Roll Call five times a day whether in camp or on the march any man missing roll call three times in succession without leave of absence from a Brigade or Major General is to be put in irons sent to the rear of the army his horse and arms to be taken from him and he put into the nearest Infantry regt from his state and other instances where they are absent without leave for a few days they are to be considered deserters and shot accordingly I have heard nothing from Saml. & John in a good while I have not been able to learn yet whether Phifers Brigade is with this army or not there are however about ten thousand of Vandorns men at and about Columbia they had a fight near Franklin some time ago in which there were some twenty two or three hundred prisoners taken and report has it that we lost about one hundred men killed wounded and missing about thirty of them killed. There has been some Skirmishing a long the picket lines but with the exception of the fight at Fosterville on the half way ground Shelbyville and Murfresboro and Vandorn there has been none of any consequence since the battle of Murfresboro I heard some time ago of the fall of Arkansas Ft[1] but did not know until lately that any of our boys were captured there We have heard from Felix Kennedy and Wm Slaughter since I wrote last they were taken prisoners at Murfresboro and at some point as they were on their way North each of them met a brother who had been taken at Arkansas post = I suppose they will be exchanged soon if it has not already been done.

There will no doubt be an important move here in a short time Forage is getting very scarce in the vicinity of the army and it is very hard to get in some places atall in fact considerable Districts are destitute and it has to be hauled to them from a considerable distance

There is therefore a necessity for a move and if Providence spares me until I see the move through all its course I will write you what it is =Write as often as convenient and let me know all about home and things thereabout I would like very much to see grand pa again I saw cous J L Webb a few days ago he and family were in good health they are at a Mr Kings about four miles from here now but it is hard to get an opportunity to go to see them. Cous J^{ns} say he is going to Texas when I go out after the war = May the Almighty grant us the privilege= Yours in filial regard &

C.W. Love

I learned a day or two ago that uncle Andrew was at home by a letter from Elizabeth written to John and Sam but directed through mistake to me.

1. Fort Hindman, a Confederate fort on the Arkansas River near the town of Arkansas Post. Confederate brigadier general Thomas Churchill surrendered the fort on January 11, 1863, ending the Battle of Arkansas Post. Cyrus's brother

James was a part of that fight, as James writes about in Letter 57.

Letter 65

Shelbyville
Tenn

Apl 19th 1863
Ja[s]. M. & T A Loves:

Dear parents:

I wrote about the time I left Unionville down in the S.W. Cor of Bedford County which I think was about three weeks ago I am still well except Diarrhoea which does not seem to be any better than for some time past. the last I knew of Terry Wilie was when I left the wagons at Unionville he was not entirely well at that time but not worse than myself and would have been with us but for his horse not being able to stand the trip—. the Limestone County boys generally are in good health except Diarrhoea which is common among our Reg[t] no doubt on account of the kind of diet we have to eat which is nothing but bacon and bread= no vegetables of any kind except as we can get them from the citizens which is hard to do as there are so many cavalry all over the country and things of this kind scarce

Sam and Joe Bake are with Vandorn at Spring Hill between Columbia and Franklin Sam wrote to me that John had been left in Miss—when they started up here and was unwell at the time= he had not heard from him and did not know but that the Yankees had got him or that he may have died=I hope not the latter but want you to write any thing you may have learned about him. I want to know also any thing you may know about Ja[s]. I saw cousin John Webb before we left Unionville he and family were at Cousin Jas Marshals a son I think of old Gilbert Marshal= There are three of them Ja[s], John & Rob[t] living at or near a little place called

Chapel Hill= Their uncle old John Marshall lives in Franklin= there are several other Marshals living near Franklin= Cousin John Webb has been married twice= his last wifes virgin name was Norris (Margaret Norris) their oldest child is a daughter Elizabeth the next a boy Amasa then Margaret, then another little boy whose name I have forgotten and their baby, Jas Hunter = Cousin John is rather lying out from home as by staying at home he is in great danger of being taken by the enemy and if recognized by those who were at Murfresboro last year he is in danger of being hung a thing which they threatened to do if they could get him when they took Old uncle Amasa = There are a great many unionists in nearly all parts of this state many of them became reporters when the enemy were in here last year=some one of whom reported that old uncle Amasa hauled some Confederate soldiers from his house down to Shelbyville on which account they took him prisoner and kept him there till he died

We went up near Nashville about ten days ago and about five hundred went down to the R.R. between Nashville and Murfresboro captured a train & destroyed it and also about one hundred of the enemy after killing some thirty or forty= the boys among them got some thirty or forty thousand dollars in green backs[1]= another party went to the Cumberland river where the Railroad runs under the bank of the River and shot an engine to pieces and possibly killed some stock on the train another party went across toward Boling Green and captured two telegraph batteries another went to Harts=ville killed four Yankees and captured fifteen together with a suttlerwagon which was loaded with good things to eat drink and wear. ^and also about 50 head of beef cattle^ we have heard that the Yankees were advancing from Nashville and also from Murfresboro for the purpose of attacking us but whether it is so or not I cannot tell since this is the second day since (according to report) they should have been here. they certainly know our strength and will not be likely to come unless with a large force of both infantry and cavalry—Felix Kennedy and Wm Slaughter who were taken prisoners at Murfresboro have been exchanged and are now back at the Brigad wagons.

Nothing of importance to write

Yours with filial regard &c
C.W. Love

1. This is an extraordinary sum, equivalent to between $500,000 and $750,000 in 2015 currency.

Letter 66

Cyrus Love, as the schoolteacher in the family, typically has the best penmanship, spelling, and grammar of the Love brothers. There are quite a few atypical spelling errors in this letter, possibly due to time constraints or grief, as the content reveals some familial losses.

The Virginia battle Cyrus describes toward the end of the letter is probably the Battle of Fredericksburg, fought December 11 through December 15, 1862. Considered a Confederate victory, it was one of the bloodiest battles of the war: Confederate forces under Robert E. Lee lost 4,500 men, but the Union's casualties totaled 13,300.

Sparta
White County Tenn
May 14th A.D. 1863
Ja^{s} M & T A Loves:

Dear parents:

At this as at all other times I take pleasure in writing to you. but the is some information lately received by Mark Perry which I had not had any intimation of from any of you in fact Theressas last letter stated that

Jas[1] was in pretty good health but from Marcus Perry I learn that he is dead but my mind has been prepared ever since we came out in the war to hear of the death of any of my folks but I have hoped always that the hour of death would be the hour of happiness to them

I was paied to learn of Ellens lingering in such pain for so long a time before she died but at heart I am prepared to say the will of the Lord be done It may be you will be afflicted by the loss of more of your children before the war is over or they they may loose you without the opportunity of again seeing your faces on earth but what ever the Lords will may be with us here let us live so that we may be happy together in Eternity where our Redeemer dwells.

I have heard nothing particular about the death of either Ellen or Jas but I hope some of you will write particulars when you write again.— This leaves me in the enjoyment of very good health except bad cold.

The Limestone County boys generally may be said to be in good health and are cheerful enough generally would that I could say they would get back home with hearts no worse stained with immoralities than when they left but this can hardly be said of any in the army of but very few at most th Temptations to gamble drink Whiskey and swear seem to almost irresistible to most men in the Confederate army but the great evil among them is the influence of bad women of whom there are a great many throughout the hills and mountains of Tenn

It is really heart sickening to see how ignorant and debased these people living as they do without any effort to make themselves better have become there is not one out of every ten I do not believe that can read and write but there are of course some very honorable exceptions to this and some excellent and intelligent people live here. the extensive character of vice among the women is no doubt owing to their ignorance they are therefore to be pitied but when the Governor— or rather the Legislature of the State has a chance to operate freely again they ought to adopt measures to force them to educate their children.

Terry Wilie is still driving a wagon as his horse is not able to do service. Our horses generally are in bad condition as there is no forage in this country and what we have has to be brought from forty to fifty miles on their backs. We got into camp yesturday evening after having been off to the corn country some eight or ten days I carried over half a bushel of corn back with me and my horse seems to be badly jaded this morning as the fruits of it there are however many worse than mine

We are to be paid off again to day— I have spent all the money I ever drew since I have been in the service for clothing tobacco and something to eat. I do not desire to save money through this war all I want with it is to get plenty to eat drink and wear and if I can have these by spending my money for them so long as the war lasts I will be satisfied I have had just about what I needed for this purpose since I have been in service by the help of the $100. 00 sent to Uncle A C. L by uncle D. H. L. that served to get me a horse and saddle and I have been well supplied with everything needed in clothing line since I have been out by buying instead of drawing from the government. The army generally seems to well clothed well supplied and in good spirits

You have or will no doubt hear of the result of the various fights that have taken place lately=Forest with seven hundred men captured sixteen hundred and killed some two or three hundred down near Rome Georgia a short time back—they were a body of the enemy[s] cavalry going to Rome to destroy the gun factories there but before they got there the citizens met and repulsed them Forest then came on them and captured nearly if not all of them.

There has been an=other severe fight in Va in which we are reported to have whipped the enemy badly=the fight took place some where near Fredericksburg on the Rappahannock River= it is reported in camp how it got there I do not know that 10,000 prisoners had been brought in to

Richmond= Stone Wall Jacksons arm badly hurt by a shot from some of our own men and one of the Hills A.P. I think slightly wounded the fighting has been severe and losses heavy on both sides.

We have as yet no account of a termination of the fight nor do I know how long they had fought up to the time of last accounts I heard some one of the boys in camp say this morning that a Nashville paper puplished that Hooker would do well if he got away with half of his army.

I suppose you knew that Ge^{nl} Morgan married his second wife a Miss Ready of Murfresboro a short time before the fight at Murfresboro—since then he has been staying with his wife and apparently neglecting his duties as an officer until within a few days past he called all his troops together went up some where to the North of this near Livingston and attacked and whipped a large force of the enemy taking a good many prisoners I suppose from what I have learned that it may be counted a considerable victory.

I have not heard from our left wing in some time and do not know how the boys are—I have however the news from there that Vandorn has been killed by a Dr. Peters and if all I have heard be true Peters ought to have killed him. The difficulty was on account of liberties taken by Vandorn with Peters wife.[2]

Nothing more now

Write to me often.

My best wishes for all of you=The Almighty protect us

Yours with filial regard &c
C W Love

1. Cyrus refers to his brother James, also known as Jim throughout the collection, who we speculate has died of disease.

2. Van Dorn was shot in the back of the head on May 7, 1863, by Dr. James Bodie Peters, who claimed that Van Dorn had an extramarital affair with his wife, Jessie McKissack Peters. Peters was arrested by authorities but never

brought to trial.

Letter 67

Rutherford Co. Tenn

June 12th A.D. 1863
Ja^{s} M & T.A. Loves:

Dear parents:

This leaves myself and the other Limestone County boys of this Reg^{t} in tolerable good health one of them however (Felix Kennedy) who was taken prisoner at Murfresboro took Typhoid fever and has not been well since. There are at the present time of the Limestone County boys in this Regt S. K. Skruggs. Wm Lynch. Dick Oliver. Terry Wilie. Felix Kennedy. Walter Wood. U Posey. Wm Slaughter Wm Perry. Marcus Perry. Robt Brooks. Pete Kendall. Thos Burney. Wm Owen. and myself. Griffin Kennedy has not been with us in the capacity of a soldier since we took Murfresboro he was wounded at that time and it has made a cripple of him for life (I mean the fight of last year) he is at this time down about Columbia Felix Kennedy has not been well since he was taken to Camp Chase. The Company to which I now belong numbers about forty men A M [Shannon] Capt. J W Baylor 1st Lieut and S. K. Scruggs 2nd Lieut

You have no doubt heard from the 7th Texas oftener than I have and consequently know more about it than I do It seems from the accounts I have of the fights before Jackson Miss that the 7th Texas and 6th Tenn brought on the fight and it seems also that Genl Gregg was in command of the forces there I have not learned with what stubbornness our boys fought or what their losses were

There has been but little and in fact almost no fighting here since the Murfresboro battle except what has been done by Vandorn and Forrest on the left.

You have no doubt learned of the death of Vandorn and that Forrest is now ocupying his place as commander of the forces on the left of this army=he lately drove the enemy out of Franklin and occupyed the place himself for something near a day but the enemy got reinforcements from some two other places and drove him back again= It seems there is a man by tho name of Jackson in command of a brigade of Texas Troops who have been sent from Forrests command to Miss to the army Johnson is concentrating there but I do not know whether the reg[t] to which S.B.. J.W. L[s] belong had gone down there or not if so I do not calculate on being able to hear from them in a good while. The Arkansas Post prisoners are here at and about Beach Grove and Fairfield Harry Prender.. and other of the Limestone County boys are here but not in very good Health or spirts I have not seen Harry as yet but expect to see him in a day or two if nothing comes in the way more than I know of at the present time= Crops are very fine in this country and will make an abundant yield in most places but in others there is a good deal of Smut[1]= Things are now as they have been for some time dull and of no importance. I had not learned of James[s] death till the arrival of Marcus Perry I have said some things in this letter that I said in a former letter but from the uncertainty of their getting to your hand[s] I have concluded to repeat them.

I hope the blessings of Almighty will attend you and protect us both so that we may meet again.

Yours in filial regard &c
C.W. Love

1. A parasitic fungi causing disease in cereal grasses.

Letter 68

Wartrace Bedford Co Tenn}
June 18th 1863 }
Jas M & T A Loves:

Dear parents:

I wrote a letter a letter a day or so ago to be taken to Texas from the Ranger Regt. but I am now H D Prendergast having come down to see him yesturday the regt he belongs to now is a consolidation of the 6th 10th &15th but it is said to be only a Temporary one. I find here a good many men I did not expect to find at this place. there are capt. Bennett H. D. Prender John Lynn Joe Tyus J J [DeBorde] Milton Tucker and some others many of whom you do not know= they do not seem to be pleased with the idea of being kept at this place the think they ought to be allowed to go west of the Mississippi. There are a good many of them affected with diarrhoea but none of them dangerous

The Rangers are to be moved from where they are at this time down farther toward the left of the army possibly to old Middleton where we picketed first after the fight at Murfresboro and near where cousin JW Webb lives= if we go there I will write to you again soon as I shall then be able to see him again= We may go to Chapel Hill farther west but I will write from there as I do not know of any thing to hinder= I have learned that Uncle A C is back to the old Regt again= he was with these boys at Arkansas post for some time there is nothing of importance going on about this army There does not seem to me to be any intention on the part of either army to advance=We have nothing but bad news from Vicksburg reports have been on the wing for several days that the place has been captured but I do not believe it. Grant has a large army aroun the place and is besieging it very closely but I do not think he can take it by storm or otherwise till Johnson will have a sufficient force to drive him out there is as I have said no news of any importance here and I will not undertake to write any more

I would like very much to have some word from you as I have had none in some time.

Yours in fillial regard &c
C W Love

Letter 69

In the following letter Sam describes hearing gunfire from the besieged Vicksburg, about thirty miles away from his position in Brownsville, Mississippi. He also describes the recapture of Winchester, Virginia, a town that changed hands several times during the war. Brigadier General Robert H. Milroy's Union troops occupied Winchester from the first of January, 1863, until Major General Richard Ewell's Second Corps retook the town in mid-June, capturing between 2,500 and 4,000 Union troops.

Brownsville Miss. June the 29th / 63

Dear Father & Mother

There is a gentleman going to start up to Texas tomorrow morning who will carry letters for us and as there is no chance for us to send a letter home unless we send it by hand ~~and~~ we have to avail ourselves of every opportunity that we have. John & I & all the other Limestone boys are well. John had an attack of the Dropsey[1] but he is entirely well of it now.

Our horses are looking well and we have plenty to feed them on.

There is but little news here of interest for there is not any fighting going on here except at Vicksburg= they are shelling each other there more or less every day. We can hear the guns very distinctly. The firing sometimes is very havy though it is said they do little or no damage to our fortifications.

Th^e^y have made several attacks on the line of fortifications since they have been here but met with a terrible repulse every time and they will met with no better fate if they were to attempt it an hundred times oftener Tehe yanks admit the loss of from 60,000 to 65,000 men in the different attacks on Vicksburg and Fort Hudson and there is no doubt that they have lossed a great many from disease for the citizens in this country say that they are in the sickliest country they ever saw and the sickly season has just commenced add to this that the water is very scarce so very much so that they have to drink out of mud holes or bring all their water from the Miss river or the Big Black which is not much better than the water from the mud puddles after it is hauled 15 or 20 miles through the hot sun. We have all confidence in Johnston and if there is another man in the world that can keep his plans as profoundly a secret as him I would like to see him——There is not a man that knows anything about his plans unless it is his corpse commanders and that is very questionable at present.

We have been on several small scouts in the last week but have not effected anything though we come very near running on their infantry last friday before we knew there was any infantry there for the first we knew of it was by hearing their drums between a ¾ of a mile and a mile off beating a call to arms—We listened a while and then turned back about half a mile. The yanks thought they would have a good thing of it for they had sent a brigade of cavalry up the road late the evening before and they thought we would go down it to get a peep at the webfoot and they{{the cav=}} would come up in our rear but they were mistaken= The cav. Videtts[2] were looking at us all the time for they fired on our advance guard as soon as we started back but hurt no one our boys returned the fire and held their place for some time. After we had fell back about half a mile we stopped and offered the ~~the~~ Cav.. battle but they would not accept though ther was but one Reg^{t}.. and one battalion of us and a Brigade of them.

I have but little else to write abut the army here through our arms have met with a signal success in Va.. at Winchester. Gen. Ewell commanding Jacksons old corpse captured Gen.. Milroy with 7,000 or 8,000 men. When Ewell demanded the surrender of the place Milroy told him that if he was attacked he would burn every house in the place Ewell repyed that if did he would hang every yank in the town. Milroy didn.t burn the town. I is also reported that Gen. Lee is advancing into Pa.. at the h^e^ad of 90,000 soldiers. I do.nt know whether it is reliable or not though it is certain that Gen.. Stuart has made a successfus raid in to that state. Hooker it is reported is trying to get in a head of him.

I will now have to close by sending my love to you and mother and all the friends and request you to send this to Bettie for when I write a letter to one I want it to be considered to all for I cannot write to all every time I write. I received a letter from Cyrus it was written about the first of May.. he was in remarkably good health.

Tell Bettie not to get mad because I donot write her a separately letter. And Fred I aught to answer his letter but I cannot now. I would have answered it sooner but I could not. Tell him to read this letter and consider it headed Fo Mr. Fred Karner[3] and then write an answer for I like to receiv letters from my stay at home friend.

And now with filial regards I remain your son Sam..

It is rumored that you are going to elect Sam Huston[4] governor of Texas and that he is going to try to set up a seperate nationality and call the Texas troops home if he does we will come home and ha^n^g as a cowardly traitor we hope he will not be elected for we consider him an unsound man[5]

Robert Marshall Love

1. Dropsy, or edema, is an abnormal accumulation of fluid in a body's tissues.

2. A mounted soldier positioned beyond an army's outposts to observe the movements of the enemy.

3. John Karner's brother.

4. A Unionist, Houston had been deposed as Governor in March 1861 when he refused to take an oath of allegiance to the Confederacy. He died a month after this letter was written, casting doubt on rumors of his imminent election.

5. This postscript was written at the top of the first page for lack of space.

Letter 70

In camp near Brownsvill
June the 29th 1863

Dear Sister

As I have written everything that would be of any interest in fathers letter my principle object in writing to you is to send my love to a few special friends for after writing father I will have little else to write to you but I cannot conveniently send a message of love or respect in his letters to the girls

Give my love to Nannie Serena and Mollie and tell Mollie and Serena that I would have wrote to them if I had not written several letters to them since receiving theirs. In one of mine I proposed to write to them as often as I had an opportunity of doing so if they would do the same[1] but I have not received an answer and I do.nt know whether they will do it or not but I can write to you and Nannie= for this is for her too= and you can ~~th~~ tell S.. & M.. that I still think of them. Tell Lou K[2] that I would like to hear of her Give her my Love kiss her and box her on the cheek once for me. Tea as I said I have nothing to write so I will have to close soon.

Write often and write long letters for I love to read lond one[s] if I donot write long ones and tell all others to do the same. I received the letter you sent by Capt.. Ross. I was glad to hear from Texas for I considered the news cheering.

Tell Robert I am glad to hear of him giving so much for hospital fund and also tell him that he can do mor that way than he could in the army for he is too young to stand it.

Give my love to all and reserve to yourself a large portion Sam

1. See, for example, Letter 20.
2. Possibly Lou Karner, Mary Elizabeth's daughter.

Letter 71

Between these letters the two most significant battles of the Civil War occurred, both of which gave advantage to the Union and together marked a turning point in the war. In the eastern theater, the Battle of Gettysburg was fought from July 1-4, 1863, ending in a Confederate retreat. In the western theater, Vicksburg surrendered to Grant on July 4, 1863. As the letters reveal, morale among Confederate troops suffered in the wake of these losses. In Letter 72, Sam writes about the problem of desertions in the Confederate army. Estimates of Confederate desertion are as high as 100,000 men, though the total is almost certainly many fewer due to a mislabeling of soldiers as deserters who were later discovered to be wounded, captured, or merely temporarily absent. For more information see Desertion During the Civil War *by Ella Lonn.*

In the summer of 1863, Cyrus is in Tennessee, and Sam and John are in Mississippi under General Joseph E. Johnston. Though they were not involved in the Battle of Vicksburg, Sam indicates in Letter 69 that he and John were close to the action. The postscript of this letter is written by W. A. Blaine, presumably a friend of John Karner and perhaps one of the Limestone County boys.

{{In camp near Morton Mss.
July the 22st 1863

Dear sister[1] I have an opportunity of writing you a few lines to let you know that I am in good health and doing very well. We are not having much fighting at this time. John is not well though he is not atall dangerous. He never will be well in the service though I intend to keep him in the country and <u>never</u> let him go to a hospital. Joe.. & Tom.. are in fine health. There is but little news of importance to write to you and if there was I would not have time to write it. Mr. Karner is here. He is in good health. Col.. Moody was dangerously wounded at the battle of Jackson= The ball entered low down under the Spine ~~the~~ ranging towards his hip. Mr Karner was a little unwell when he first got here but he is perfectly well at present he will start home in about two weeks and if he succeeds in crossing the river he will be at home in about six weeks but do not look for him until you see him or be anxious for he ~~w~~ will be shure to get there some time. Mr Karner says for you to keep the children close and not let Johnny go to the Tank.[2] Cy was in fine health the last time I heard from him. Mr Karner sends his love to all and you may give mine to Lou Fred[3] and all other enquiring friends. Bettie send this to father as soon as you can with these few hastily written lines I remain your brother

Sam

P..S.. Pete Lewis and all the other Limestone boys are well

Mrs. Karner
With Mr. Karner's [permission] I add a [hasty] P.S. don't feel any uneasyiness about Mr. Karner. He is in good health & spirits. none of us are down in the mouth over the fall of V. Burg nor will be so long as the memory of loved ones at home has a place in our [?] harts & especially we boys who think of the young ladies we left behind. Kiss them all for me & present my kindest regards to them & all my [body] of [relatives] my kindest respects to Mis Lou & Miss Emma [rember] me to [Betty] & Johnny and [accept] the kindest [assurances] of your

Friend
[W. A. Blaine]

1. In the letter, Sam identifies the recipient as Bettie (Mary Elizabeth Karner).

2. "Tank" is a colloquialism used by farmers and ranchers to describe a farm pond.

3. Lou and Fred are Bettie's children and Sam's niece and nephew.

Letter 72

{In Camp 12 miles from Brandon
{August the 7th 1863

Dear Sister

There has been an order from Gen.. Johnston allowing one man out of every twenty five a furlough to go home or they allow all to go home but those living on the west side of the ~~of~~ Miss River.. but they have given furloughs to several of our boys and they are going home at their own risk. They were drawn for and I was not fortunate enough to get one. Tea.. I have but little ~~of~~ news to write except what you have already heard.. Everything looks very gloomy at present ~~T~~ though I have a faith in the Justice of our cause that makes ^ me^ think that we will come out all right yet.

There is one thing that causes everything to look more gloomy than the mere success of ^the enemy^ it is the disertion from our army.

A very large number of our men have diserted in the last two months and it is going to make the service a great deal harder on those that are left. The disertion has been principly confined to the States of Miss.. Ala.. Tenn.. & N..C.. though there has been more or less of it among all the state troops. Texas has had less than any of the States though there has been several disertions from our Regt.. and Whitfields Brigade in the last six weeks. If ~~instead~~ all had stay— and done their duty like men instead of diserting our "Subjugation would have ^been^ a matter of impossibility for the f^a^rthere they advance into our country the more men they will have to detach from their main force to protect their communication.. for our cavalry would keep the R..R.. torn up all the time if they did not keep very strong guards at all the points and while it would be widening their force it would be concentrating ours.

I will simply state that Gen.. Lee got the worst of a heavy battle in Pa and has retreated back to Va the extent of his loss is not known here though there is no doubt it is very heavy. Gen.. John H Morgan and all his command went into Indiana and burned a great deal of government stores and it is reported with some degree of certainty that they were all captured at least it is generally believed.[1] I do not know whether Cy was with him or not.. he was with Wheeler the last time I heard from him and I am in hopes that he is with him yet.

Tea.. as I stated at the outset ^that^ I ^ have^ but little to write that would be interesting and my letter will have to be a short one. I might ~~tell~~ ^write^ you a long letter about things that are so trifling that they would not interest you or anyone else.

We are lying in camps and are likely to do so for some time yet though it does not agree with me to do so for though I do not get sick I donot feel as well as when we are on the march

John is able to be in camps again and I am in hopes he will continue so I have more hopes of him now than I have [?][2] had in 8 or 9 months.

Joe.. Tom..Pete and all the other Limestone boys are in tolerably good health.

Tea.. I want you to write me how everything is getting along in the country generally and send it to by some one of those that are furloughed

I will try to get Lt.. McAnn to come by Fathers as he is going home. There is one thing I had like to have forgot. You stated in your last letter that you had heard of something that I had been guilty of "Some misconduct that was disgraceful I would ~~not~~ like to know what it is for I am not aware of anything that I have done that would have disgraced me at hom even. I would also like to know who was the <u>kind</u> informant. Whoever it was was better informed than I was for I was not aware of it. There are a few men in our ranks that will do almost any thing and they at times become almost a disgrace to the Reg[t].. For myself I have endevored to do nothing that I would be ashamed of here after.

Tea give my Love to Nannie and tell her that I would be glad to receive a few lines from her. Give my Love to Mollie Serena and Lou. The reason I do not write to any of them is because I have written several times since receiving any word from them. I will expect a letter from Mollie and Serena when the boys come back.

Give my Love to all the family and relations and tell Fannie to write to me for I have not forgotten her and I want her to consider my letters as much to her as any one of the family

I will now have to close by sending my love to you and all the others of the relatives and friend

Your brother Sam..

..S.. To Mother

Pete rode in to the country and bought some of the finest [peper] I ever saw in my life. The pods are as large as a Teacup and I send you some in Tea[s] letter

If you think you can send us clothing this winter let us know. As we will not buy if you attempt to send us some.

Write by the bearer. S.B.L. [pr] A A L

1. From June 11 to July 26, 1863, Confederate brigadier general John Hunt Morgan led a group of nearly 2,500 Confederate cavalry into Union territory in Kentucky, Indiana, and Ohio. As Sam's letter suggests, the raid was highly publicized. Morgan surrendered in northern Ohio, but eventually escaped and returned to the South.

2. A letter is marked out here.

Letter 73

The letter contains a matching envelope addressed to "Jas M. Love Springfield Limestone County Texas."

Near Rome Geo
Aug 15th 1863
Jas M & T.A. Loves:

Dear parents:

It has been some time since I wrote to you but you will have no doubt heard from by the letters from the other boys in the Regt as they have been writing all the time and I have requested them to write so you could hear from me. We are all in tolerable good health here. There are however some small complaints [among] the boys. Dick Oliver has been afflicted for a long time with [risings] brought about by Vaccination[1] in his case as in many others the vaccinated part makes a bad sore first rising of an equally severe character come under the [arm] and else where about on the arm and body until they finally lay a man up and in some instances it has become necessary to take the arm off to save the patient Wm Lynch has been afflicted with tooth ache for several days past all the other Limestone Co boys are in good health Terry Wilie as you have no doubt learned before now was taken prisoner while we were crossing the Mountains and we have heard nothing of him since. There is a good deal of sickness in the Regt but none of it that may be called serious. I have heard nothing from Saml & John for four or five months they are somewhere in Miss if their lives have been spare to this time you no doubt have news from them frequently. S.K. Scruggs got a note from [Harry] prender a day or two back he is at Chattanooga all were well I learn from men who are just down from Tennessee that the the enemy there are ravaging the country as badly as a set of vandals would the have taken all the wheat in the country and moved it into their quarters and every man who does not take an oath to aid our enemies against us his property is confiscated and he put in prison. The Almighty certainly holds a severe punishment over the heads of all such nations of people we no doubt deserve all the punishment we have received since the war begun but I have no more doubt now than at first of the final establishment of the Confederate Government

I have learned of the death of James Jo[s] Douglas and Ed. Scruggs but have learned nothing from John W since Sam[l]. B. left him in Miss. the last information direct from Sam[l] was while they were at Springhill Tenn. but I have heard from them since then and even since they went to Miss again I have heard from the brigade that it was healthy but have nothing from the boys—We have no news of importance here that can be relied on as to what is going on between the two armies. We have heard that Mead was reinforced by Grant and Rosencrans with the view of overpowering Lee before he could be reinforced we have also a report that none of Grants army are above Memphis. reports show that but little is being done about Charleston. there is no doubt I think of the fact that Morgan and a part of his forces have been captured in Ohio and Indiana. the Yankee report up to the last accounts I saw were that they had captured between four and five hundred. We have accounts of some things said to have taken place with the forces of Gen[l].. Pegram who went with about three thousand men into Kentucky a short time ago. they are said to have had some successes and some reverses nothing however definite from them. It is also reported that another big fight is about to take place in Va. and that our forces feel confident of gaining another victory whenever the fight does come on I thought for a while that Grant would try to throw his forces in by Mobile so as to get behind Johnson if possible. but from what I have learned lately this cannot well be done as the country above Mobile is of such a character that an army cannot be moved in that direction.

I have heard nothing from cousin John Webb since I left his house just as we began the retreat from Tennessee. I have tried hard to ascertain something about Uncle Harvy Braden but have not in all my enquiries been able to find a man from that part of Ala in which he is said to live.

We are here now for the purpose of recruiting our horses and may remain here till some time in Sept but there is no chance to know definitely how long we will remain at any place. I am still with the Rangers and do not know whether I will go back to the old regt at all I have not had a letter from any of you in a long time write as soon as you can your &

C.W Love

1. The process for administering vaccinations was often painful and unsanitary. Doctors would make several cuts in a patient's arm and then administer a small amount of vaccine directly into the wounds.

Letter 74

The last letter written by Cyrus comes from Rome, Georgia, just before the Chickamauga Campaign, a series of battles fought in northwestern Georgia in August and September 1863. At this time, the Union army under General William S. Rosecrans pressed toward Atlanta, opposed by Bragg's Army of Tennessee.

{South of Rome Geo—
{August 20th A.D. 1863
{Jas. M. & T A Loves:

Dear parents:

I wrote a letter to you the other day but have since learned of a more reliable opportunity of getting one to ^you^ through the favor of a capt. Ashby who from some reorganization of his regiment has been displaced in consequence of which ^he^ has resigned and is going home—some of the boys who have had an acquaintance with him say he will do to rely on and I therefore prepare this in hopes that of the two you may be able to get one.

This leaves myself and the Limestone County boys who are here in tolerable good health. Terry Wilie as I stated in my other letter was captured as we were coming out of Tenn a portion of Wolfords Ky Cavary followed us up on Cumberland Mountain where we had a fight with them they killed one of our men and wounded several others but none of them mortally our scouts followed them back to or near the foot of the Mountain and they learned from some persons living in a house a mile or two back of where we had the fight that we killed three of their officers a Co^{l}.. Lieut.. Co^{l}.. and a Lieut..and also eight privates. There appears from the best information that we can get to have been three Reg^{ts} of the enemy who expected as we learned from one of their number who was captured during the fight to find some of the troops from these old states to be on picket who are much easyer as a common thing to surprise than those who like ourselves have been somewat accustomed to watching. our regiment was however on picket and to make every thing more secure a double set of pickets were put on the same road which is the only practicable road up the Mountain from Winchester toward Bridgeport the fight took place near the sight of Southern University[1] which was talked of so much just before the war began. The enemy were close on our first pickets before they could be seen his gun missed fire but the cap popped and was heard at the picket base who were ready to mount in an instant as soon as the enemy saw the first picket they began to charge and by the time the men at the first picket base were mounted they were among them: oweing to our guns having been wet by the rain of the day previous very few if any of the guns at the first base fired. They fell back to the second base the enemy coming up almost at the same time at this place a few more guns fired than at the first they all together then fell back to the Reg^{t} where the different squadrons were formed at different places one of them was formed on a small wastefield of two or three acre[s] in size the Squadron composed of two of about the largest companies in the Reg[t] another Squadron was formed about one hundred and fifty yds behing them and just outside of the field the squadron to which I belong was formed behind some bushes nearly parallel with the road which at this place runs nearly East and West and on the North side of the field: the enemy charged the squadron in the field and were met and repulsed twice by charges from the squadron. there were however three Reg[ts] of the enemy who after their repulse began such flank movements as forced us to fall back. we had two pickets out on our right flank as we started to move of Terry Wilie was sent to call them in but could not find them very readily as they had left their posts and started back at the time the squadron did Terry was by this detained so long that the enemy got right on him—and from what I can learn although I believe Terry started toward us his horse was shot down and he captured—a gentleman in another company says he heard the enemy halting some one of our men and that who-ever it was told the yankee not to shoot that his horse was killed I myself heard some one hollowing halt and supposing it was some of our Officers tried for a few moments but on turning back to look I saw that it was the enemy as I could distinctly see or rather understand by the yankee brogue and by the bullets whistling by me

We fell back then tolerably rapidly to form behind the 4th Tenn Reg[t] they wer in line and when the enemy had got in about One Hundred twenty or thirty yds of them they turned loose a tremendous volley of balls in the direction of the enemy who finding that our forces were increasing as we fell back wisely concluded to make their way back to the foot of the Mountain which they did in considerable haste leaving some of their dead behind them. as our scouts ascertained who followed back in their rear till they started down the Mountain there was as the scouts learned eleven of them killed and about thirty wounded besides several horses killed. we had as I said before one man killed and not over three or four wounded and only one of them badly and was brought along to this side of the Tennessee River and was getting well the last I heard from him we had several horses wounded in our Reg[t] some of which had to be left just as we got behind the 4th Tenn Reg[t] some careless fellow caused a gun to go off and kill a fine horse in their lines this was the only horse killed in the Confederate lines that I knew of during the fight two horses in our company were wounded one of them belonged to Bulger Peeples. I do not know whether I said so in my other letter but I will say here that my life has again been protected by Providence when the enemy first began to advance our Reg[t] & the Eleventh Texas fought them on the pike between Murfresboro and Shelbyville and while loading my gun after firing a ball cut the brim of my hat in about an inch and a half of my face It has been the will of Deity that I should not be killed so far and I hope He will protect my life through the war so that I may be able to return to you—The sum of my wishes for some time past is that I may live to get back to you but as I set in for the war I will continue in it to the end unless disabled so as not to be able to do service in which case if I can I will come to the West of the Mississippi where I can hear from you oftener

The enemy are in the The Tenn River below Chattanooga about Bridgeport. there has been considerable cannonading at this place between our forces and those of the enemy at this place but I have heard of nothing resulting from it to either side We can get no news from Virginia Charleston or Mississippi of a reliable character there are some few fights between our Cavalry and that of the enemys in Va also some of the same kind in West Tenn and Miss. They are also doing the best they can to take Charleston but so far as I have been able to learn they are making but slow progress toward taking it both sides are still hard at work making fortifications: I do not believe they will succeed in taking it atall as the loss of Vicksburg has taught our Commanders that Fortifications must be well provisioned and have plenty of amunition and they can hold out and I would jude from the way we are stinted in provisions at the present time the Government must be giving Charleston plenty to supply them for some time!

We are getting about ¼ pt rice & about 1 oz sugar pr week: 1/3 lb hog in the shape of bacon bulk pork or pickled pork and about the same of beef. plenty of cornmeal and flour and whatever we can get in the country is what we have to live on our money however has gin out and we therefore will have to live pretty hard until we ar paid again which will be some time off as it has not been long since we were payd.[2]

There is plenty of provisions of all kinds in the country.

I have not heard from Sam[l] & John since about the time they left Tenn You no doubt hear from them oftener than I do: I heard from H.D. Prender a few days ago all were well then

I would like very much indeed to hear from you: if you have any chace write Dave Prender came this side the Miss but did not get here but some of the letters he brought came to hand. I have not learned whether you wrote by him or not (U Posey on account of a difference with his Officers and the sentence of a court Martial to dig holes as a punishment for not being at roll call because the bugle was not blown and not going on extra when ordered has) left the Regt) and I expect will not return

—Tell Tenny. Alice. Mary. Lizzie and Johy K to be good children and study hard.

Yours with filial regard &c
C.W Love

Send this to the relatives around about

1. Sewanee University, in Sewanee Tennessee, founded in 1857.

2. The typical rations of a Confederate soldier consisted of hard tack, beans, beef, and coffee, often supplemented by foraging, as Cyrus notes in this letter.

Letter 75

By the beginning of 1864, the Union army had begun to tighten its noose around the Confederacy. Since victory at Vicksburg in July 1863 had given the North control of the Mississippi River, Union forces had been pushing east through Mississippi; Grant had taken Chattanooga and had designs on Atlanta. In the eastern theater, Lee's army had retreated into Virginia after its defeat at Gettysburg, with the Army of the Potomac under General George Meade close on his tail. As this letter notes, Sam and John were primarily involved in rear-guard skirmishes in western Tennessee and northern Mississippi, outside these major conflicts.

The following is a combination of two fragments in the Love family letters. The first part is the beginning of a letter with at least a page missing. Although this part is unsigned, the handwriting and style indicate that Sam is the author. Added to this is an undated fragment, also written by Sam. It has been placed with the dated portion of the letter, since both discuss Texas. The undated fragment is labeled below.

Madison Station Miss..
Jany the 13th /64
Miss Tea.. Love

Dear sister

For the first time in about three months I attempt to write you a few lines; but I donot know whether I will get through with it or not for my pen is so bad.

There is but little news of importance=We have had several fights since I wrote to you last & one tolerably hard fight at Moscow on the Memphis of Charleston R.R. it lasted about ¾ of an hour we killed drowned & captured about 150 men and 200 horses. We wer fighting on the bank of Wolf river=we came very near capturing their battery=We lost 29 killed & wounded 8 being killed. The 1st Miss and 6th Tex.. fought the 6th, 7th, & 9th & Iow ^Ill^ & 2nd Iowa and a section of a battery {{2 guns}} we whipped them quick & fast the 6th Tex.. & the 6th & 9th Ill..~~and the~~ and the 1st Miss and the 7th Ill & 2 Iowa run together= we captured all the horses of the 6th & 9 Ill.. though we did.nt get them all off= I did.nt get a horse. Though I might have had [?][1] pick and chois for I was the first man that got among them though it is my misfortune never to get any thing that way for instead of getting horses or other property I always continue to fight untill it is too late to get any=thing= When I first run on the end of the bridge the yanks.. were just leaving the other end and were ~~seren~~ screening themselves from the fire of the main portion of the Regt. behind a leevee that was thrown up for the road= when I got on the end of the bridge I fired on them about 20 paces and then run under the bridge to reload and there were three yanks there= they surrendered to me and give me 2 six shooters and as soon as I got my gun loaded I leveled it on another and he threw up his hands and told me not to shoot that he would surrender I then told him to come to me= And directly afterwards the command was given to fall back and I instead of bringing out a horse brought the 4 prisoners & they came very near getting me twice as I came out for just as we started they opened on us with grape canister & shell & minnie ball and the prisoners begged me to let them stop behind trees but I made them keep on until I got so tiard that I had to stop myself= they fell down behind logs & I jumped behind a large [poplar] tree & I had.nt more than got behind it before a shell struck the ground about 2 feet from me & covered me nearly up in dirt= I thought that a piece of the shell had hit me at first: but fortunately it did not burst= if it had bursted it would have killed me outright. ~~Though~~ I came out all right prisoners & all. I give one of the six shooters to Joe.. P.. and the others. to John Joe lost his.

Tea I got a pass a few days before Christmas and went to Dr. ~~Z~~ Zolicoffers and stayed there until after new year= I spent the time very pleas=antly and formed the acquaintance of a number of young Ladies & several young gentlemen.

Though I met with the misfortune to loose two of my blankets & a negro I think must have hit my horse with a rock or stick and fractured his skull so that I had to leave him the next day after I left Dr. Zs. he may recover though I think it doubtful.

Tell Cousin Sallie that all of he relatives are well & that the property of her Father has been divided & that Charels & Susana I believe felt to her= there will also be some money comeing to her though I do.nt know how much.

Tea I hear a grea deal about Texas and the soldiers that have been back there are very much dissaisfyed with the conduct of the citizens of the state generally and although I attribute a great deal of it to the soldiers being disappointed in their expectations there must be some fault with ~~th~~ the citizens. They say that the citizens have lost their patriotism

[undated fragment]

And that they are extortionous in their charges for everything they do and that they do it grudgingly= now if this is [?][2] true it is bad for I had fondly [?][3] hoped that Texas would not be wanting in patriotism. I have not been there nor do I know whether I will ever be there to judge for myself or not.

There is a great deal of tak of the Teh Texas Regts on this side of the river bursting [?][4] up & going home at the expiration of their term of service and I hope that the citizens of the state will discourage it as much as possible for if one states troops go home the others will have the same right

Tea..I will have to close as it is getting late and I have to carry it several hundred yds to the gentleman that is going to ~~bring~~ ^take^ it across the river

Tea.. cousin Guss Zolicoffer told me she was going to write to you= Letters may be sent from this side of the river by directing them via Meridian & from that side via Alexandria or Shrevesport I am not shure which. All the boys are in good health John Pete & Joe ~~are off on~~ have been off on a scout but they are comeing back and we leave our camps tomorrow morning to go and meet them. Give my love to all the family and relations and to Nannie and Serena and I would send my love to Mollie if I was not afraid her spouse would be jealous. I will now close with the kindest regards of your brother

Sam..

P..S.. Write soon and tell all to write

1. A word is marked out here.
2. A letter is marked out here.
3. A letter is marked out here.
4. A letter is marked out here.

Letter 76

Benton Mi.. Jany.. the 22nd 1/64

Dear Father and Mother

It is with great sorrow that I attempt to write you a few lines for I have just heard of Cyrus being killed or wounded and I have just written to Wm Lynch to know if he can tell me any thing about him. I have requested him to let me know where the fight took place also to know if he has heard anything of him since he was shot.[1]

I see in the letter that Pete received from his grand pa that Wm Lynch was also reported to be missing but he came in for I saw him myself he & Felix Kennedy were together= They came to our camps while we were in Ala.. and stayed siveral hours. He had been off on a pass to get his horse and could not get to his command until after the report that was published was made out.

There is but little news of importance in this or the Va.. department. About the only news that I know of is the expe=dition of our brigade to the Mi. river during Christmas and new year for the purpose of crossing money & guns[2] to Gen.. Smith^{s} army.. it was the coldest weather ever known in this ^country^ so the the old citizens say and the boys had to cross the river during the night and work in the mud and water until their feet were frostbit. It was the worst expedition this Brig. has ever been on. John ~~nor~~ ^and ^ I ~~was~~ were not on it John went to the sunflower on the west side of the Yazzoo river and was left there on picket until the command returned and I was off from them getting me some clothes at Dr Zolicoffer^{s} and did not know that the command was gone until it had been gone several days

Perhaps you have not heard of the fight at Moscow.. on the Memphis & Charleston R.R. it took place on the 4th of last month.. the reg^{ts}.. engaged on our side were the 1st Mi.. and the 6th Texas on the side of the yanks was the 6th, 7th, & 9 Ill.. & the 2nd Iowa.. the first Mi.. engaging the 7th Ill.. & 2nd Iowa while the 6th Texas engaged the 6th and 9th Ill…

We whipped them very bad killing wounding capturing about 150 of them & killing drowning and capturing about 200 horses.

We at one time had possession of all the horses of the 6th & 9th Ill.. & might have brought them off if we had commenced as soon as we got possession of them.. but instead of that some come out with horses whilst others were fighting & I was one of those that continued to fight so that I got no horse. The result is I have had to buy one of those that were captured.

Instead of bringing off a horse I brought out 4 prisoners and came very near loosing my life for as a I was comeing out a shell struck the ground in about 2 feet of me and came very near knocking me down with the dirt=.. but fortunately it did not burst or I believe it would have killed me.

After going about 10 steps farther a shell bursted som 10 or 12 feet above my head and a piece of it came within a half foot of hitting me on the head..it struck the ground in 6 or 8 inches of my feet. The yank prisoners begged me to let them lie down behind logs but I told them that had as good a chance to escape as I had and they must go on. And now while I am speaking ~~to~~ about the battle & horses it reminds me that I bought the horse from Frank Jackson a son of old Hesikiah Jackson & agreed to pay him in cows and ~~Ka~~ calvs to be delivered to his Father next spring.

The reason I done it was because I was affot my horse having died about 2 weeks since and the money we get will hardly keep us in tobacco so that it is nearly impossible for us to get clothes for the citizens on this side of the river do.nt care much for a Texas soldier and we have to pay enormous prices for everything we get. we have generally made out for cloteing this winter but I donot know what we are to do next winter for our money is going down every day[3] while the price of everything is going up so that if [Janes][4] remains at the present price it would cost us $200 for a suit of [Janes] to say nothing of shoes shirts & drawers.[5]

I promised to let Jackson have 7 cows & calvs for the horse I bought from him.

I will have to <u>close</u> for I have nothing else to write.

Give my love to all the family and the relations and all enquiring friend.

With these few lines I remain yours with filial regards

Sam Love

1. According to the company muster roll, Cyrus was killed on October 7 at the Battle of Farmington, Tennessee.

2. "&guns" is written vertically in the margin on the left hand side of the page.

3. Privates were paid, generally, eleven dollars each month, although Confederate paydays often ran as much as six months in backlog.

4. Possibly jeans, not made of denim, but a short-waisted jacket and trousers made of a blend of wool and cotton threads.

5. At the time of this writing, Confederate inflation had reached a high of seven hundred percent.

Letter 77

This letter is written in pencil, which may indicate that supplies were running low.

Camp near Dover[1]
{Mach the 3st of 64

Dear Sister

I have an opportunity of writing you a few lines.

We are in fine health and doing very well at present.. pete has not returned from the river yet.. though we are looking for him every day.

I have nothing to write of any interest only I want you to tell Robert to stay at home until he is of age & then come to me before he joins the service atall and I will get him in a company of scouts commanded by Capt. Sam Henderson brother of Wm Henderson of Corsicana and by all means tell him not to join the company that Cobb will be trying to make up for he is not the man I would like for Robt.. to be under but if he will do as I tell him he will get into the <u>very</u> <u>best</u> arm of the service and with an officer that will respect him.

Tell Robert that he had better stay at school as long as he can.

Tea Gen Lee says he is going to furlough every [?] man[2].. if he does I may get a furlough this year some time if I live long enough.

I will have to close this hasty letter

Give my love to pa & ma.. and the ~~{children}~~ other members of the family and tell them to write to me.

My love also to Lou Nannie & Serena & to yourself the love of your Brother, Sam

P.S. John has gone a fox hunting with a citizen.

1. Likely Dover, Tennessee, near the Kentucky border.

2. In January 1864, General Lee issued an order offering a furlough to every soldier who would procure an able-bodied recruit.

Letter 78

{In camp near Tuscaloosa Ala..
{Aprile the 27th /64
J. M. & T.A. Love

Dear father & mother

I have commenced to write but I hardly know what to write about for there is a good deal to write about and I hav.nt time to write as much as I would like to. We have had a row with the Col.. of our reg^{t}.. his name is Wharton and a lower down man it would be hard to imagin and we were determined to have nothing to do with him.

Gens Lee & Jackson were determined to force him on us until they found that we were as determined as they were..and now they are trying to get rid of him by cashiering[1] him=.. After they found that force would.nt do they ishued an order disgracing the whole reg^{t}..and had it read to all the reg^{ts}.. in the corpse but all the other Miss.. reg^{ts}.. are anxious to be with the 6th yet & while I was in the artist galery yesterday having my likeness taken Gen..Ross & Col..Pinson of the 1^{s}t Miss.. were in there for the same purpose & Gen. Ross in reply to Col.. Pinson= asking him if he was going to get a furlough said that he would not get one. but if it had.nt been for trouble in the 6th he would have got off .. Col .. P .. told him (Ross) to send the 6th back with the 1st Miss.. and they would take care of us and we would have no trouble.. in reply Gen.. Ross said that if we were back with him, we would need no one to take care of us.. signifying that we would be perfectly satisfied as we were rid of old Jack and would then be with our favorite regt.. the 1st Miss & I will here say that there is not a more gallant Col.. in the Confederate service than Pinson or a more gallant regt.. in the C.S.A. than the 1st Miss.

In reference to the orders disgracing us I will only give one instance of the many hundred of what the citizens in Miss.. think of it.

I was taking Supper with a family shortly after the occurrence.. And while supper was preparing I was talking with a couple of young ladies {{ members of the family that I formed the acquaintance of }} about the order & they told me that we need.nt be uneasy about that for every one thought we had done right.. and shortly after an order was read to us from Gen. Jackson complimenting us very high.. but he thought he was going to have some fighting.

There is one thing that you are may not be aware of that will be a little gratifying to Texas citizens.. it is that this is the most distinguished Cavalry brigade on this side of the Miss river & I do.nt suppose that any on that side would claim equality.

This will appear egotistical but it is not written in that spirit.

The yanks & negros have a perfect horror for us the negros especially for we have killed about 400 of them in the last 3 months.. besides we have killed since the Moscow fight[2]..that fight included about 300 yanks and captured about 200.

They are talking about furloughing this brig.. by regts.. & Gen.. Lee has written to Gen.. Polk to know if he must commence now.. the 3d will be furloughed first & the 6th next. If they commence soon you may look for the 6th about Aug.. or Sept & me with it if nothing happens to me between now and then. We are all in fine health. Pete has returned from the Miss river & I had like to have forgot to tell you of the attempt to murder Dr Zollicoffer mad by a diserter..the Dr was called to his galery late at night and shot in the stomach about 4 weeks since and the last time I heard from him it was not known whether he would get well or not. The Dr had the day before told a man that he had no corn for diserters and it is believed that he done it. I will have to close. I send you my likeness John is not here to have his taken or I would send his with mine. He is with Lt. Col. Pete Ross in Walker co after diserters. Give my Love to all the family & relations & all enquiring friends.

With these I am with filial regards your Son Sam.

P.S. Tell Maj.. Boyd that Pete is not here or he would write..but he is well

1. The dismissal of a disgraced military officer.

2. The Battle of Moscow, Tennessee was a small skirmish that occurred on December 4, 1863. This was one of the first battles in which African American troops were used on the Union side.

Letter 79

This letter appears to be hastily written; the handwriting, in pencil, is faint and messy. Although the year is illegible, Sam's account is probably a confused version of events at the Battle of Kennesaw Mountain in Georgia, which took place June 27, 1864. What became known as Cheatham Hill, named after Confederate major general Benjamin F. Cheatham, was held by the Confederates with great loss of life on the Union side. "Cleborn" probably refers to Confederate major general Patrick R. Cleburne. The Battle of Kennesaw Mountain was considered a Confederate victory.

June the 28 .. 6. [?]

Hard fighting and with artilery and small arms= Charged Cheatham Cleborn Hindman= Got possession of Cheathams Works= drove back immediately= Cleborns Div.. Stood as firm as a rock= killed 7 of Cheatham men with bayonets = Good many Yanks killed with bayonets= Hav.nt.. seen .. report..[?][1] = rumor says several thousand Yanks killed & wounded =saw [2] Ganbury^{s} Brig= said very small loss = Saw train cars with 64 Yanks prisoners several 100 more captured= very heavy Skirmishing along the entire line= Furguson.s cowardly Brigade run & F did not tell Ross of it= Yanks flanked Ross before he new it & he but he come off with the loss of 10 men= Ross Brigade is very confident of whipping if the other Brig^{s}.. will stand by them= Pete is sick= he ~~is~~ has the Bronchitus= he is tolerably sick though not dangerous he went to the hospital yesterday= his ma.. need..nt be under any aprehension for him for I think he will be well in a week or ten days. I am taking care of his horse.

Tea I received the letter that you sent by Cobb yesterday evening & you stated that the reason Robt.. did not join Coobbs Co.. was that he was gone after Fannie. That is the least & smallest reason why he should not Join the co. for I wrote you a letter & sent it by Cobb himself geiving Robt every reason that any body could why he should not join that co.. & if he will not take my advice after 3 years of rough experience & a fair chance to judge of the characters ~~of~~ & dispositions of men especially a man that I have been as clocely connected with as I have been with Cobb.

Cobb is a brave man.. but [?][2] that is the only qualification he has for an officer= he is the most tyranni^c^le man I ever saw & notwithstanding he has had a good deal of success he fights without any judgement.. & the consequence will be that one of these days.. him & his men will all be ~~ca~~ captured or killed [sometime] through his want of Judgement & besides that if Robt is determined to come in to the service before he is of age he might ~~waig~~ wait until I can come home (if I ever do) for I will come this this fall if ever get a furlough & then I could have got him into [any] place where he could have done well= & Tea. I want to know whether you got it or not as soon as you have an opportunity of writing to me.. & by all all means tell Robt.. to stay at home until fall.. for I will repeat what I have already wrote to ~~Robt~~ him that the service is something he knows nothing atall about & it does seem to me that ~~Robt~~ he ought to have confidence enough in me to take my advice.. and advantage of the experience that 3 years of hard service has given me.. but if he will not do it let him go & do as he will. Yours in haste Sam

1. A word is marked out here.
2. A word is marked out here.

Letter 80

The letter is written shortly before the fall of Atlanta, which occurred on September 1, 1864. During the time this letter was written, Atlanta was under siege by Sherman's army. The letter is written on one page and is folded to construct an envelope. The envelope is addressed to "Miss Tea Love Tiwacany Hills, Texas." The words "Due 10" indicates that the postage was not completely paid by the sender as was customary. However, it is post stamped "Fairfield Tx," indicating that the postage was paid by the recipient.

Atlanta Aug.. the 11th /64

Dear Sister

I am at the 7th on a visit for the purpose of seeing Col..Moody= he wrote me a note yesterday = evening stating that Robt.. & Button had crossed the river with him but had been separated from them = he says that Button was a little sick & Robt.. was waiting him = he says that they will be on in a few days. I am anxious to see them. I shall try to get Robt with a co of Scouts. They were in Miss..when he left them. Tea we are all safe yet we have had a good deal of fighting & several men killed or wounded though none of our co.. our chaplain was serious if not mortally wounded while tending the wounded = We were after a raid commanded by McCook of about 3,000 men.. We captured about 1,200 men & 1,500 to 1,800 horses 21 ambulances & 2 pieces of artilery= Tea if you can let the friends of Co G, know how they ^are^ getting on= I might write you a long letter but I hav.nt the time— Give my love to all the family & relations & all enquiring friends & the best affections of your brother

Sam..

Letter 81

This entry is composed of two letters written with pencil on one piece of paper. On the front is a letter from John; the letter on back is unsigned, but is in the style of Sam. Both letters have portions that are so faded they cannot be read. Only the legible parts have been transcribed here. The addressee of John's letter is unclear, though it is likely he is writing his father. The words "Robert arrived here" can be made out in the first few lines of his letter. Confederate records indicate that R.M. Love joined Company C of the Sixth Texas Cavalry.

Camp near Atlanta Aug 20/64

They were charging through a lane & I was holding horses about one hundred yards out in an ~~a~~ old field ~~I~~ they began to shoot at me & the rest of the horse~~s~~ holders so we took with leaving got all our horses & every thing else belonging to our co I have a splendid Horse though he belongs to the C S A. I think we will whip these ~~yan~~ Yanks here at Atlanta Wheeler has gone to the rear & we hear that he has torn the R. R. up from Resacca[1] to [Tunnell] Moutane[2] & has blown up the the Tunnell[3] & has gone to fortifying himself we hear that he has enough troops to whip all the yanke [cavl] in this department

There is a great many rumors about our getting furloughs this fall I am in hopes we may get them & come home alive once but if fate is against us & we have to stay I intend to stay here until I can come home honorably for a dersertir now has no claim ~~to~~ on any ones sympathy—I believe that we will come this fall that is if this fight ever gets over good love to [Tea] & all the family respects to all enquiring friends

Your son John

Dear Father & Mother

I have but little news to write except I should tell you about the recent raid & I suppose John has told you all about it however I will say this much that after fighting the yanks one day & a half they met the infantry & they stopped them & we came up behind them & attacked them The Infantry quit fighting as soon as ^we^ attacked in their rear & they (the yanks) ~~th~~ turned their whole attention to our brig.. & with about four thousand men they run over our brig.. of about four hundred. but we continued to killed them untill they all passed. We killed & wounded about 5 to one we lost one gun of our battery & captured one gun & [2] fags from them th^e^y got a few of our horses. Gen. Kilpatrick told two cit,s that he did not expect to whip Ross brig.. but he was going to run over it with overwhelming numbers.. & he done it but he did not make anything for he lost a good many men & horses while he was at it for the b^o^ys all faught like bull dogs killing & wounding a great many after they commenced passing us. = Gen.. Wheeler has been in their rear 12 or 15 days & the understanding here is that he is going to stay there if the yanks do not reinforce enough to whip him & it is th general impression here that Gen.. Sherman will have to attack soon or go back to Chattanooga.

There is

1. Resaca, Georgia.

2. Refers to a town called Tunnel Hill in northwest Georgia.

3. A nearly 1,500 foot long railroad tunnel that runs through Chetoogeta Mountain.

Letter 82

Written after the Civil War ended in 1865, the letter describes the activities of the Love family women, particularly in matters of courtship. With the possible exception of Letter 4, this is the only time we see a letter written by one of the Love sisters, though their presence has been felt throughout the entire collection. The letter is merely signed "T," but it is likely Tea, who according to one available record, did not marry until 1870. The letter reveals "T's" personality, as she is playful, makes fun of her advancing years (she is well into the years considered to be marriageable), and often utilizes sarcasm. It makes no mention of the war, but instead focuses on courtship and weddings, leaving the reader with a sense of hope for the Love family, despite its losses, as well as for the South in general, proving life goes on.

"Loves. Retreat=" March. 13th 66

Miss Fannie Farnsworth,[1]

Cousin Fannie,

I have been thinking ever since the boys got home that I would write to you, but I thought you might have written to me first had you been really desirous of having me show my ignorance in letter writing

Truth to tell Cousin I am so rusty that it is an exceedingly irksome task for me to write now. It was once the only pleasure I ever really felt, but age is creeping over me now and with it comes stiff joints, scattered thoughts, and a restlessness that will hardly admit of my being still long enough to write, or rather to collect my wandering thoughts. I hope Coz you will receive these excuses as a sufficient apology for a badly written and [loosely] connected letter.

Everything is dull, and everybody are something on the same order. Billy and Buddie (Bob)[2] are just starting on a hunt. It has been raining all day until within the last half.hour it has ceased, and the hunters are in a perfect fever to start a wild cat. George is staying with Mr. Robertson, [though] I presume "the boys" have told you of this. He has not been to see us since he went down there. We look for him every Saturday, but we are disappointed every time

Sammie White has left us and gone over east I was sorry to see him leave. He is a nice boy and quite ~~handsome~~ handsome (a greater attraction for me than moral worth) Mr Duff — I hardly know how to spend my opinion about him. He hardly spoke to me the whole time he staid with us. I tried my very levelest to make an impression but dear me he I seem to know ~~I~~ that I was wreathing my face in smiles purposely for his benefit — I invoked Cupid in my behalf — but the little Elfin would not undertake to pierce his heart for me and I therefore gave up in despair, hoping that the sweet disturber– Love would never visit him. I am quite positive Iir is one Love who will never disturb his peace of mind— that one is myself.

Thanks Cousin for the present sent by Buddie. I appreciate the gift coming from you I am very much afraid the good lessons taught in The Wedding[3] but will be wholy thrown away on me. however I am studying it closely and am learning my duty to my better-half and if I should ever be wheedled into marrying Ill know my duty— yes and hisn too— for it not only instructs the wife how she is to do, but [ ]t gives the "Lords of Creation" a general sweep.[4] A strict line of demarkation is placed between the duties of each, but one is no less severe than the other. I I must stop w'iting, for I've already got your head in a perfect whirl, owing to my jumping from one subject to ano"her without ""aking a look". Present my kindest regards to all your friends. I Give my love to Cousin Mary Uncle Sam, Aunt Nancy, and the rest Write to me soon Cousin and I will Ily immediatly to your letters I wrote to you several years ago — (when I was a novice in the art of letterwriting) but never received a reply to my letter— supposed you had failed to figger it out and consequently determined to trouble you no more Theirs a young lady near you that Buddie is dreadful bad off about. I think her name is Lyda or Lydie— Tell her that I think if Buddie gets no better of his ailment she will have to answer an all important question soon Im merely warning her.

Good by Cousin

Ever thine
T. Love

1. Margaret Frances "Fannie" Farnsworth, daughter of Nancy Gorden Braden and Samuel Hill Farnsworth.

2. Possibly a reference to T's younger brother Robert.

3. Presumably a wedding guide.

4. Written tongue in cheek, a possible reference to Ephesians 5:22-23 or First Corinthians 7:39. Both passages provide instruction on how both men and women are to treat each other within the confines of a marriage.

Epilogue

IN POSTBELLUM YEARS the Loves returned to prosperity and became a prominent family in Limestone County. The last letter in the collection is probably penned by Tea, who writes to her cousin Fannie, just a year after the war has ended. However, like the other female-authored letters, this letter barely mentions the war at all, offering only a vague reference to the war's end: "I have been thinking ever since the boys got home that I would write to you" *(Letter 82)*. However, the letter's contents move quickly to a discussion of a potential beau and her studies in the art of courtship and marriage, which have been enhanced by a recent gift from Fannie: "Thanks Cousin for the present sent by Buddie. I appreciate the gift coming from you Im very much afraid the good lessons taught in The Wedding but will be wholy thrown away on me. however I am studying it closely and am learning my duty to my better-half." The letter may seem insignificant in content, but corroborates Harrison's view:

> Whether encouraged by traditional Southern culture, influenced by the presence of their men returned home, or compelled by the hardships and need within their domestic setting, numerous white women diarists encouraged themselves in the contexts of immediate defeat not even to write about their political interests but to define postwar roles in reference to family, religion, and self-improvement within domestic contexts. (2013, 150)

In other words, the end of the war signaled a return to domesticity and a hope for the preservation of traditional ways, including the expectation of marriage and children. Once more the choice to remain silent on the subject of the war could be a coping mechanism, a way for the women to reassure themselves that life will resume as normal. On the surface, anyway, it appears the Love women have done just that.

According to Mansfield, the men turned to law enforcement: first, the father James, who as sheriff was killed "from ambush in 1873"; later, John, who that year "took up arms once again in behalf of constitutional rights" when, along with his deputy Robert, he "stood with pistols bared at the foot and head of the stairs of the State Capitol and protected the members of the legislature . . . enabling them to organize and administer the oath of office" to the newly elected governor of the state; and finally Robert, the deputy who succeeded John after John was "killed by escaped prisoners" (2000, 66). Robert, drawing on this experience as well as his (exaggerated) Confederate career, became something of a political star, eventually ascending to the office of state comptroller of public accounts.

Two additional letters, from the private collection of Louise Burton, are found in the appendix and are written by Robert to his cousin George Washington Farnsworth from his desk in Austin, Texas. In his letters he mentions seeing his siblings Tea and Sam, proof that the family still maintained close contact and communication after the war. Ending the collection with Robert's letters provides a nice symmetry to the collection as a whole, as readers see in the first letter Cyrus's instruction to his younger brother to focus on his education, and Robert's words in the last letters indicate that Cyrus's words were not in vain, since it appears that Robert is now overseeing the school that Cyrus and his brother-in-law began. He assures his cousin, "The school is doing nicely" *(see appendix)*. Robert's success after the war, no doubt, would have been a great source of pride for Cyrus, but while Robert survived his few months in the war, he was violently "assassinated . . . by a disgruntled ex-employee" on June 20, 1903 (Mansfield 2000, 66). The photograph of Robert at his desk in Austin is supposedly the last taken of him, mere minutes before his death.

Robert Love at desk.

Even at the moment of his death, Robert asked that his murderer be forgiven (Mansfield 2000, 66). *The Dallas Morning News* article accompanying the collection writes, of the Loves, that "a better family of people has never lived," though "there has been a singular line of fatality among them" (July 1, 1903, 2). Hale and hearty Sam finally passed away on March 25, 1912, "at the age of seventy-four in Fort Worth, Texas, where descendants of the brothers live today" (Mansfield 2000, 66). In all, the chronicle of Love family correspondence is exceptional for its depth and breadth and richness of material, as well as its remarkable preservation in the Special Collections archive of the Mary Couts Burnett Library at Texas Christian University.

Appendix

Although not designated within the corpus of the Love family letters, a number of related documents emerged during our research that may be of interest to the reader. In addition to copies of poems and popular songs of the day, there were two post-Civil War letters, generously donated from Love descendant, Louise Burton, which were penned by Robert Love to his cousin George Farnsworth during Robert's time in office. We append these letters in the hope that they allow readers additional access to the Loves' world.

This letter is written on stationery with the official letterhead of the state comptroller. It contains a Texas state seal on the right hand side. Robert is likely writing from the same desk where he was later shot.

Comptroller's Office
Texas

R.M. Love
Comptroller
J.H. Walker
Chief Clerk[2]

Austin, Sept 6th 190_[1]

Mr George W. Farnsworth,
Lockney, Texas

Dear Cousin,

Your food of August 16th came to me abt six days since just as I was leaving for Tehuocana was your five days [hence] the delay in answering sooner The [Sour] county school land is now in Lilingoton, the [atly] [?] is geting in shope to bring out [vs] the U.S. for all amt of money [T.C.] & pended by Tx as an hour Co—also the school land. He has just gotten authority from a joint resolution passed by both branches of the legislature to withdraw all necessary papers from this office for the purpose of bringing out I sent to the land [offering] refund that there is no map of Budy [Love] [Courters] My wife is at Tehuacana for a short time I went up took Ruth T Entred her in school Aunt Bettie Prendergast still living Mr. Karner died some 10 or 15 days since the school is doing nicely the question of removal will be settled next week at [Tynod] which [meets] at Hillsborro on 12th just I would write you at length but am [pressed] with business, all well at house office work moving smoothly—Bill [Horthorn] (Col) and wife are here I gave Bill a place as porter he is the same coon that he was at Tehuawna—love to all relations and friends

Your Cousin
R.M. Love

1. Robert did not fill in the blank for the year.

2. The names and titles are part of a letterhead that also includes the state seal of Texas.

George Washington Farnsworth

Comptroller's Department Oct. 8th 1901
State of Texas Mr. G.W.
Farnsworth
Austin

R.M. Love, Comptroller
J.H. Walker, Chief Clerk.[1]

Dear Cousin—your [?] of 3rd Sept came to my office during my absense. I saw the announcement of Gov [Sawyer] [?] of Joe Dickson to the place made vacant by Judge Newtons Death. So I did not get to represent your request to governor Sawyers—I came from [Lunstown] yesterday visited Sam & Tea at Richland. [Jimmie] [Croneratis] is staying at Orchland now—we like his wife quite well—Jimmie seems to be quieting down the past year—and I hope will do well—all guilt of the Hills all well at my home I have been trying to get out to see Billis grave and dress it but have not yet—I will soon I was never so [confined] as I have been since I took charge of this office. I hear from Jimmie occasionally—he hasnot been well—but is better now he suffered with ulceration of stomach & bowels—when I was at [Lubuck] & I do not thank he has or ever will recover from the effects of it. I would love to see you all. I may come up this Fall or Winter—with love to all your family & friends

I am your Cousin
R.M. Love

1. The names and titles are part of a letterhead that also includes the state seal of Texas.

Acknowledgments

FOR HELP with research, we would like to thank Roger Rainwater, Susan Swain, Lisa Pena and the rest of the TCU Special Collections staff who have supported us and patiently listened to us transcribe and proofread the letters. For her support of the project from its early stages to completion, we thank June Koelker, dean of the library. We are immeasurably grateful to our professor and mentor, Theresa Strouth Gaul, for teaching us all we know about epistolary studies, editorial methods, and archival research, and for her generosity and willingness to read drafts of our work. Without her time, energy, and support, this book would not have made it to fruition. For help obtaining and collecting valuable historical documents, we extend our gratitude to Dixie Jackson. For their generous sharing of anecdotes, photographs, and other family treasures, we especially thank the Love descendants, Louise Burton and Maureen Pierce. Several of our TCU colleagues and friends provided crucial emotional support during our work, most notably Chris Foree, Jessica Menkin Kontelis, Amanda Barnett, and James Chase Sanchez. We are very grateful to our editor, Kathy Walton, and to Dan Williams, Melinda Esco, Jensen Branscombe, and Rebecca Allen at TCU Press for guiding us through the process of our first publication.

Kassia would like to thank her parents, Dixie and Norma Jackson, for their encouragement, and to extend a special thanks to Brent Waggoner for his unflagging patience and support.

Adam would like to thank his parents, Ken and Chris Nemmers, for giving him the time and space to pursue his personal interests. A big thanks as well to Maggie McLeod, and again to James Chase Sanchez and Amanda Barnett for their support during the writing of this book.

Works Cited

Altman, Janet Gurkin. 1982. *Epistolarity: Approaches to a Form.* Columbus: Ohio State University Press.

Burke, Kenneth. 1966. *Language as Symbolic Action: Essays on Life, Literature, and Method.* Berkeley: University of California Press.

Charles, Harry K. 2012. "American Civil War Postage Due: North and South." Paper Presented at the Seventh Annual Postal History Symposium, Bellefonte, Pennsylvania, November 2-4. http://stamps.org/userfiles/file/symposium/presentations/CharlesPaper.pdf.

Clark, Edward. 1861. "Proclamation to the People of Texas" Broadside, August 26. The Gilder Lehrman Collection, The Gilder Lehrman Institute of American History, New York. http://www.gilderlehrman.org/collections/62f168f4-b4e9-407f-9bfc-098043763393?back=/mweb/search%3Fneedle%3DClark%252C%2520Edward%2520%2528fl.%25201861%2529%2526fields%3D_t301000285.

Daniel, Larry J. 2004. *Days of Glory: The Army of the Cumberland, 1861-1865.* Baton Rouge: Louisiana State University Press.

Deaton, Charles W. 2012. *The Great Texas Stamp Collection: How Some Stubborn Texas Confederate Postmasters, a Handful of Determined Texas Stamp Collectors, and a Few of the World's Greatest Philatelists Created, Discovered, and Preserved Some of the World's Most Valuable Postage Stamps.* Austin: University of Texas Press.

Decker, William Merrill. 1998. *Epistolary Practices: Letter Writing in America before Telecommunications.* Chapel Hill: University of North Carolina Press.

Garrison, L. R. 1915. "Administrative Problems of the Confederate Post Office Department." *Southwestern Historical Quarterly* 19 (October): 111-141.

Gaul, Theresa Strouth, and Sharon M. Harris, eds. 2009. *Letters and Cultural Transformations in the United States, 1760-1860.* Burlington, VT: Ashgate.

Gaul, Theresa Strouth, ed. 2005. *To Marry an Indian: The Marriage of Harriett Gold and Elias Boudinot in Letters, 1823-1839.* Chapel Hill: University of North Carolina Press.

Garvey, Ellen Gruber. 2013. *Writing with Scissors: American Scrapbooks from the Civil War to the Harlem Renaissance.* Oxford: Oxford University Press.

Gerber, David A. 2006. *Authors of their Lives: The Personal Correspondence of British Immigrants to North America in the Nineteenth Century.* New York: New York University Press.

Glover, Lorri. 2007. *Southern Sons: Becoming Men in the New Nation.* Baltimore: Johns Hopkins University Press.

Harrison, Kimberly. 2013. *The Rhetoric of Rebel Women: Civil War Diaries and Confederate Persuasion.* Carbondale: Southern Illinois University Press.

Johnson, Nan. 2002. *Gender and Rhetorical Space in American Life, 1866-1910.* Carbondale: Southern Illinois University Press.

Lonn, Ella. 1998 *Desertion During the Civil War.* Lincoln: University of Nebraska Press.

Love family letters, 1859-1866. Special Collections, Texas Christian University Mary Couts Library, Fort Worth, Texas.

Mansfield, Jennifer S. 2000. "Yours Fraternally Until Death: The Civil War Letters of the Brothers Love." *East Texas Historical Journal.* 38 (1): 53-70.

Murrah, Jeffrey D. 2001. *None but Texians: A History of Terry's Texas Rangers.* Fort Worth, Texas: Eakin Press.

Trelease, Allen W. 1995. *White Terror: The Ku Klux Klan Conspiracy and Southern Reconstruction.* Baton Rouge: Louisiana State University Press.

Index

About the Editors

Photo courtesy Scott Reese Visuals

Kassia Waggoner is an English PhD candidate at Texas Christian University, where she serves as women and gender studies graduate assistant and teaches American literature, women and gender studies, and composition classes. She lives in Fort Worth, Texas, with her husband Brent Waggoner.

Photo by Amanda Barnett

Adam Nemmers is a PhD candidate in English studies at Texas Christian University, where he studies American modernism, post-colonial literature, and the epic novel. Hailing from Sioux Falls, South Dakota, he currently lives in Fort Worth, Texas.